THE

JACOBITES

OF

ANGUS

1689-1746

Part One
and
Part Two

by David Dobson

CLEARFIELD

Printed for
Clearfield Company, Inc. by
Genealogical Publishing Co., Inc.
Baltimore, Maryland
1997

Reprinted for
Clearfield Company, Inc. by
Genealogical Publishing Co., Inc.
Baltimore, Maryland
1999, 2002

International Standard Book Number: 0-8063-4716-3

Made in the United States of America

THE JACOBITES OF

ANGUS

1689-1746

[Part One]

by David Dobson

INTRODUCTION

In December 1688 James VII of Scotland {James II of England and Ireland} fled to France and in April 1689 William and Mary were proclaimed in Edinburgh as King and Queen of Scotland having already been proclaimed in London. Thereafter between 1689 and 1746 several attempts were made by the supporters of the House of Stuart to restore the Stuart monarchy to the throne of Great Britain. The supporters of the House of Stuart, known as Jacobites, could be found throughout the British Isles but were most numerous, with notable exceptions, in the Highlands and the North East of Scotland particularly among those of Roman Catholic and Episcopalian persuasion. The county of Angus or Forfarshire made a significant contribution to the Jacobite armies of 1715 and 1745. In 1715 the Earl of Panmure provided a regiment of around 600 men which fought at Sheriffmuir. In October 1745 David, Lord Ogilvy, son of the Earl of Airlie raised a regiment in Angus on behalf of the House of Stuart. The 1st Battalion marched south from Edinburgh into England in 1745. Shortly after a 2nd Battalion was raised which joined the main army prior to the Battle of Falkirk in 1746. The combined strength of the two battalions has been put at 700 men. Ogilvy's Regiment, then about 500 men, took part in the Battle of Culloden in April 1746. Thereafter the regiment marched via Ruthven to Glen Clova where it disbanded.

This work attempts to identify those from the County of Angus who actively provided support for the Jacobite Cause between 1689 and 1746. It includes not only the soldiers but those civilians whose help was essential and who were subsequently tried and imprisoned by the Hanoverian authorities. The book also reveals the wide range of destinations to where many were transported to or fled after the '15 and the '45. This book is a compilation partly based on original research into manuscripts in St Andrews, Edinburgh, and London, and partly on published sources here and in the United States. Finally I would like to thank Lord Dalhousie for permission to quote from his family papers.

David Dobson
8 Lawhead Road West
St Andrews
Fife, Scotland KY16 9NE

REFERENCES

ARCHIVES

PRO   Public Record Office, London
           CO   Colonial Office
           SP   State Papers
           T   Treasury Papers

StAUL   St Andrews University Library

SRO   Scottish Record Office, Edinburgh
           CH   Church Papers
           CC   Commissariat Court
           GD   General Deposit

TRA   Tayside Regional Archives, Dundee
           TC   Dundee Town Charter Chest

PUBLICATIONS

CAT	Chronicles of Atholl and Tullibardine, John, Duke of Atholl, [Edinburgh, 1908]
CRA	Jacobite Cess Roll of Aberdeen in 1715, A. & H. Tayler, [Aberdeen 1932]
CS	Chetham Society publications
CTB	Calendar of Treasury Books, series, [London, 1904]
F	Fasti Ecclesiae Scoticanae, J. Scott, [Edinburgh, 1915-]
GK	Goteborg, Skottland och vackre Prinsen, G. Behre [Goteborg, 1982]
Goslinga	Dutch in the Caribbean and Guiana, 1688-1791. C. Goslinga, [Maastricht, 1985]
HHA	History of Arbroath, G.Hay, [Arbroath, 1876]
HM	The History of Maryland, J.T.Scharf, [Hatboro, 1879]
JAB	Jacobites of Aberdeen and Banff in the Rising of 1715, A.M. Taylor, [Aberdeen, 1934]
JP	The Jacobite Peerage, Marquis of Ruvigny & Raineval, [Edinburgh 1904]
LPR	A list of Persons concerned in the Rebellion, The Earl of Roseberry, [Edinburgh 1890]
NS	Northern Scotland, series, [Aberdeen]
OR	Muster Roll of the Forfarshire or Lord Ogilvy's Regiment, A. Mackintosh, [Forfar, 1914]
P	The Prisoners of the '45, Sir Bruce Gordon-Seton and Jean Gordon Arnot, [Edinburgh 1928]
SCP	Scottish Catholic Parents and their Children, 1701-1705, F. McDonnell, [St Andrews 1995]
SP	Scots Peerage, J.B. Paul. [Edinburgh, 1904]
SPC	Calendar of State Papers, America and the West Indies, series, [London, 1880-]
VSP	Calendar of State Papers of Virginia, series, [Richmond]

THE JACOBITES OF ANGUS
Part One [A to L]

ABBOT, JAMES, dyer in Arbroath, soldier of Ogilvy's Regiment 1745.
[OR10]

ADAM, JOHN, jr., shoemaker in Brechin, Sergeant of Ogilvy's Regiment
1745. [OR8]

ADAMSON, DAVID, chapman in Kirriemuir, soldier of Ogilvy's
Regiment 1745. [OR10]

ADAMSON, JAMES, farmer in Kingoldrum, Sergeant of Ogilvy's
Regiment 1745. [OR8]

ADAMSON, JOHN, born 1692, shoemaker in Brechin, soldier of Ogilvy's
Regiment 1745, prisoner 1746. [OR10][P2.4]

AITKEN, FRANCIS, boatman in Strathcathro, prisoner in Montrose 1746.
[P.2.6]

AITKEN, JOHN, in Strathcathro, servant to Captain Edgar, prisoner in
Montrose 1746. [P.2.6]

AIR, CHARLES, kirk officer of Kinnell, accused of recruiting for the
Jacobites in Kinnell 2.1746. [Arbroath Presbytery Records]

AIR, WILLIAM, transported from Liverpool to Virginia on the Friendship
24.5.1716, landed in Maryland 8.1716, sold as an indentured
servant to Aaron Rawlings in Maryland 20.8.1716.
[HM.387][SPC.1716.311]

AITKENHEAD, JOHN, possibly born 1719 son of John Aitkenhead and
Agnes Low, merchant in Brechin, Lieutenant of Ogilvy's Regiment
1745. [OR5]

AITON, JAMES, mason in Caldhame, Brechin, Sergeant of Ogilvy's
Regiment, 1745. [OR9]

AITON, JOHN, in Kincraig, Brechin, Sergeant of Ogilvy's Regiment
1745.[OR9]

ALDIE, DAVID, journeyman weaver in Forfar, soldier of Ogilvy's
Regiment 1745.   [OR10][LPR196]

ALEXANDER, JAMES, ploughman in Gairlaw, Lintrathen, soldier of
Ogilvy's Regiment 1745. [OR11]

ALEXANDER, JAMES, farmer in Kinnaird, prisoner 1746. [P2.6]

ALEXANDER, THOMAS, workman in Balnagarrow, Kirriemuir, soldier
of Ogilvy's   Regiment 1745. [OR11]

ALLAN, JAMES, beadle of Arbroath, suspended from duty 1716.
[HHA170]

ALLAN, JOHN, workman in Pitmody, Lintrathen, soldier of Ogilvy's
Regiment 1745. [OR11]

ALLAN, ROBERT, son of Thomas Allan in Keithock, Brechin, soldier of
Ogilvy's Regiment 1745. [OR11]

ALLAN, WILLIAM, in Panbride, soldier of Ogilvy's Regiment 1745,
prisoner in Arbroath 1746. [P.2.8]

ALLARDICE, JAMES, born 1712, son of Robert Allardice and Elizabeth
Lyon, farmer in Drums, Brechin, soldier of Ogilvy's Regiment 1745,
a prisoner in Inverness and Tilbury 1746. [OR11][P2.8]

ANDERSON, CHARLES, shoemaker in Brechin, soldier of Ogilvy's
Regiment, 1745. [OR11]

ANDERSON, DAVID, servant in Forfar, soldier of Ogilvy's Regiment
1745. [OR11]

ANDERSON, DAVID, in Eassie, soldier of Ogilvy's Regiment 1745.
[OR11]

ANDERSON, DAVID, workman in Brechin, soldier of Ogilvy's Regiment
1745. [OR11]

ANDERSON, JAMES, born 1720, son of David Anderson farmer in
Bogiehall, Lintrathen, soldier of Ogilvy's Regiment 1745.
[OR11][LPR196]

ANDERSON, JAMES, in Linross, Airlie, soldier of Ogilvy's Regiment
1745. [OR11]

ANDERSON, JAMES, fisher in Ferryden, soldier of Ogilvy's Regiment
1745. [OR11]

ANDERSON, JOHN, ploughman in Bonnyton, Maryton, soldier of
Ogilvy's Regiment 1745. [OR12]

ANDERSON, JOHN, in Nevay, Eassie, soldier of Ogilvy's Regiment
1745. [OR12]

ANDERSON, WILLIAM, soldier in Ogilvy's Regiment, prisoner at
Culloden 1746.[OR12]

ANDREW, JOHN, cottar in Cotton of Affleck, Monikie, soldier of
Ogilvy's Regiment 1745. [OR12]

ANNANDALE, JOHN, born 1720, son of John Annandale and Helen
Arnold, shoemaker in Arbroath, soldier of Ogilvy's Regiment 1745.
[OR12]

ARBUTHNOTT, ALEXANDER, of Findowrie, Captain of Panmure's
Foot, 1715. [SRO.GD45.1.201]

ARCHER, DAVID, weaver in Seggiewell, Monikie, soldier of Ogilvy's
Regiment 1745. [OR12]

ARCHER, WILLIAM, tailor in Arbroath, soldier of Ogilvy's Regiment 1745. [OR12]

ARMSTRONG, THOMAS, from Angus, soldier of Ogilvy's Regiment 1745, prisoner in Inverness and Tilbury 1746. [P2.16]

ARRAT, JAMES, of Faffarty, Glamis, Ensign of Ogilvy's Regiment 1745. [OR6][LPR196]

ARSIL, DAVID, in Kincraig, Brechin, soldier of Ogilvy's Regiment 1745, prisoner. [OR12]

AUCHENLECK, ANDREW, a prisoner in Carlisle 12.1716. [StAUL.Cheap MS.5/537]

AUCHENLECK, DAVID, vintner in Dundee, Life Guard 1745, prisoner in Dundee 1746/1747.[LPR198][P2.16]

AUCHENLECK, GILBERT, born 1693, son of the laird of Auchenleck, Ensign of Panmure's Foot, 1715. [SRO.GD45.1.201]

AUCHENLECK, HARRY, born 1696, brother of the laird of Auchenleck, Lieutenant of Panmure's Foot, 1715. [SRO.GD45.1.201]

AUCHENLECK, HARRY, Quartermaster of Panmure's Foot, 1715. [SRO.GD45.1.201]

AUCHENLECK, JOSEPH, transported from Liverpool to Antigua on the Scipio 30.3.1716. [SPC.1716.310][CTB.31.204]

AUCHENLECK, ..., Episcopal preacher in Arbirlot 1715. [HHA170]

BAILLIE, CHARLES, town baillie of Glamis, soldier of Ogilvy's Regiment 1745.[OR13][LPR200]

BAILLIE, GEORGE, born 1702, bonnetmaker in Dundee, Captain 1745, prisoner in Stirling and Carlisle 1746, transported from Liverpool to Virginia on the Gildart 24.2.1747, landed at Port North Potomac, Maryland, 5.8.1747. [P2.18][PRO.T1.328]

BAIRD, WILLIAM, gardener in Montrose, soldier of Ogilvy's Regiment 1745, prisoner in Montrose 1746. [LPR320][OR13]

BALERNO, JOHN, miller at Mill of Lour, soldier of Ogilvy's Regiment 1745. [OR14][LPR200]

BALFOUR, JAMES, Captain of Strathmore's Battalion, a prisoner in Preston 1715. [CS.V.162]

BALLINGALL, JAMES, merchant in Forfar, Ensign of Ogilvy's Regiment 1745.[OR6][LPR200]

BARCLAY, DAVID, born 1720, son of James Barclay and Isabel Butchart, brewer in Arbroath, prisoner in Stirling and Edinburgh 1746-1747. [P2.24]

BARCLAY, GEORGE, born 1730, workman in Kirriemuir, soldier in Ogilvy's Regiment 1745, prisoner in Carlisle, Chester and York, enlisted in Boscawen's Force 1748.[OR13][P2.24]

BARNET, WILLIAM, ploughman in Baikie, Kingoldrum, soldier of
Ogilvy's Regiment 1745. [OR13]

BARRY, JAMES, born 1705 son of John Barry, workman in Kingoldrum,
soldier of Ogilvy's Regiment 1745.   [OR13]

BARRY, JOHN, tailor in Clockmill, Kirriemuir, soldier of Ogilvy's
Regiment 1745.[OR13]

BATREE, HENRY, from Dundee, soldier of Ogilvy's Regiment 1745,
prisoner in Carlisle. [P2.30]

BAYER, ALLAN, from Dundee, servant to Henry Pattullo, prisoner in
Inverness and Tilbury 1746-1747. [P2.30]

BEAN, WILLIAM, mason in Forfar, soldier of Ogilvy's Regiment 1745, a
prisoner in Montrose 1746.[OR13]

BEATTIE, ANDREW, born 1717 son of Andrew Beattie and Margaret
Thomson, ropemaker in Montrose, soldier of Ogilvy's Regiment
1745 prisoner in Montrose 1746, escaped. [LPR320][OR13][P2.32]

BEATTIE, PATRICK, shipmaster in Montrose, prisoner there 1746.
[LPR320]

BELL, WILLIAM, ploughman in Kinalty, Airlie, soldier of Ogilvy's
Regiment 1745. [OR13]

BELL, WILLIAM, workman in Clockmill, Kirriemuir, soldier of Ogilvy's
Regiment 1745. [OR14]

BENNET, DAVID, in Hattonmill, Kinnell, soldier of Ogilvy's Regiment
1745. [OR14]

BIBERNY, PATRICK, mason in Dundee, soldier 1745. [LPR198]

BINNY, ALEXANDER, farmer in Newmill, Tannadice, Quartermaster of
Ogilvy's Regiment 1745. [OR8]

BIRRELL, THOMAS, merchant in Dundee, Ensign of Ogilvy's Regiment
1745 prisoner in Dundee 1746. [OR6][LPR198/351]

BLACK, DAVID, weaver in Carnoustie, soldier of Ogilvy's Regiment
1745. [OR14]

BLACK, DAVID, ploughman in Airlie, soldier of Ogilvy's Regiment 1745.
[OR14]

BLAIR, JOHN, Captain of Panmure's Foot, 1715. [SRO.GD45.1.201]

BLAIR, Dr ROBERT, physician to the Earl of Panmure, fought at
Sheriffmuir 13.11.1715, escaped via Arbroath to France. [JAB.24]

BLAIR, THOMAS, of Glassclune, Dundee, Lieutenant Colonel 1745,
escaped from Dundee to Norway, a prisoner in Bergen, later to
France. [LPR198] [OR127]

BLAIR, WILLIAM, born 1727, son of Patrick Blair, workman in Knowe
of Kingoldrum, soldier of Ogilvy's Regiment 1745. [OR14]

BLYTH, JOHN, shipmaster in Dundee, 1745. [LPR198]

BLYTH, WILLIAM, pilot in Montrose, prisoner 1746. [P2.40]

BOWAR, ALEXANDER, of Kincaldrum, {of Meathie, Inverarity,?},
Lieutenant of Ogilvy's Regiment 1745, a prisoner after Culloden,
died in Perth prison 1746. [OR4][LPR200][P2.44][cf.SCP21]

BOWIE, ALLAN, servant to H. Patullo in Dundee, soldier of Ogilvy's
Regiment 1745, prisoner in London.[OR14][LPR198]

BOWMAN, JAMES, in Brechin, soldier of Ogilvy's Regiment 1745.
[OR14]

BRAND, ROBERT, merchant in Montrose, prisoner in Montrose and
Stirling 1746-1747. [P2.48]

BROCAS, GEORGE, schoolmaster in St Vigeans, suspended from duty
1716. [HHA170]

BROWN, ANDREW, born 1707, farmer in Dunnichen, transported from
Liverpool to Virginia on the Gildart 24.2.1747, landed at Port
North Potomac, Maryland, 5.8.1747. [P.2.52][PRO.T1.328]

BROWN, DAVID, in Kirriemuir, soldier of Ogilvy's Regiment 1745.
[OR14]

BROWN, JAMES, tailor in Dundee, soldier of Ogilvy's Regiment 1745, a
prisoner in Dundee. [OR15]

BROWN, JAMES, weaver in Easter Kinnordy, Kirriemuir, soldier of
Ogilvy's Regiment 1745. [OR15]

BROWN, JAMES, ploughman in Walflat, Glamis, soldier of Ogilvy's
Regiment 1745.   [OR15][LPR200]

BROWN, JAMES, baillie in Forfar, prisoner in Forfar and Montrose
1746-1747. [P2.52]

BROWN, JOHN, tenant farmer in Bolshan, Kinnell, Lieutenant of Ogilvy's
Regiment 1745. [HHA175][OR4]

BROWN, JOHN, jr., merchant in Dundee, 1745, prisoner in Dundee.
[LPR198]

BRUCE, ANDREW, born 1727, son of Patrick Bruce, ploughman in
Braideston, Airlie, soldier of Ogilvy's Regiment 1745. [OR15]

BRUCE, DAVID, born 1717, son of George Bruce and Elizabeth Will,
butcher in Brechin, soldier of Ogilvy's Regiment 1745, a prisoner in
Brechin and Montrose 1746-1747.[OR15][P2.54]

BRUCE, GEORGE, butcher in Brechin, Sergeant Major of Ogilvy's
Regiment 1745, surrendered after Culloden. [OR9]

BRUCE, JAMES, weaver in Dundee, soldier of Ogilvy's Regiment 1745,
prisoner in Stirling and Edinburgh 1746-1747. [P2.56]

BRUCE, JAMES, butcher in Brechin, son of Sergeant George Bruce,
soldier of Ogilvy's Regiment 1745, prisoner in Inverness and
Tilbury. [OR15][P2.56]

BRUCE, JOHN, butcher in Brechin, soldier of Ogilvy's Regiment 1745.
[OR15]

BRYAN, JOHN, in Montrose, soldier of Ogilvy's Regiment 1745. [OR15]

BUCHAN, DAVID, ploughman in Milton of Glen Esk, soldier of Ogilvy's Regiment 1745. [OR15]

BURN, ..., son of Mrs Burn innkeeper in Broughty Ferry, soldier in Ogilvy's Regiment 1745. [OR15]

BURNES, JOHN, Lieutenant in Strathmore's Battalion, a prisoner in Preston 1715. [CS.V.162]

BUTCHART, DAVID, ploughman in Pitskelly, Barry, soldier of Ogilvy's Regiment 1745, prisoner in Arbroath 1746. [OR16][LPR198]

BUTCHART, PATRICK, blacksmith in Benvie, soldier of Ogilvy's Regiment 1745. [OR16][LPR198]

CABLE, DAVID, born 1729, son of Alexander Cable, servant in Forfar, soldier of Ogilvy's Regiment 1745. [OR16]

CAIRD, JAMES, ploughman in Balcathie, Arbirlot, soldier of Ogilvy's Regiment 1745, prisoner in Arbroath 1746-1747. [OR16][P2.66]

CAIRNCROSS, THOMAS, workman in Kingoldrum, soldier of Ogilvy's Regiment 1745. [OR16]

CAMPBELL, WILLIAM, seaman in Carsegownie, Aberlemno. Lieutenant of Ogilvy's Regiment 1745, a prisoner. [OR4]

CANDOW, JOHN, ploughman in Longdrum, Lintrathen, soldier of Ogilvy's Regiment 1745. [OR16]

CARGILL, JOHN, a ploughman in Braidston, Airlie, soldier of Ogilvy's Regiment 1745. [OR16]

CARGILL, WILLIAM, born 13.5.1726 son of James Cargill and Elizabeth Ramsay in Montrose, a tobacconist in Montrose, transported from Liverpool on the Gildart 24.2.1747, arrived at Port North Potomac, Maryland, 5.8.1747. [P.2.324/98][PRO.T1.328]

CARNEGIE, ALEXANDER, of Balnamoon, a prisoner in Carlisle 12.1716. [StAUL.Cheap MS.5/537]

CARNEGIE, ALEXANDER, born 16.10.1705 son of Robert Carnegie and Janet Blair in Arbroath, a labourer in Brechin, transported 22.4.1747 from Liverpool to Virginia on the Johnson, arrived in Port Oxford, Maryland, 5.8.1747. [P.2.100][PRO.T1.328]

CARNEGIE, CHARLES, son of the late Sheriff Depute, Lieutenant of Panmure's Foot, 1715, to Lille 1716. [SRO.GD45.1.201]

CARNEGIE, CHARLES, sailor in Montrose, prisoner there 1746. [LPR320]

CARNEGIE, DAVID, Cavalry officer, refugee in Sweden 1746. [GK111]

CARNEGIE, GEORGE, born 18.11.1726, son of Sir John Carnegie of Pittarrow and Mary Burnett, apprentice merchant in Montrose, prisoner there 1746, escaped to Gothenburg 1746, returned to Scotland 1765, died 1786. [GK111][NS.7.1.23/145][LPR320]

CARNEGY, JAMES, Earl of Southesk, born 4.4.1692 son of Charles Carnegie and Mary Maitland, fought at Sheriffmuir 13.11.1715, escaped to France. [JAB.189]

CARNEGY, JAMES, of Finaven, Captain of Panmure's Foot, 1715, imprisoned at Carlisle 12.1716.[StAUL.Cheap MS, 5/537] [SRO.GD45.1.201]

CARNEGIE, JAMES, surgeon, fought at Sheriffmuir, possibly a prisoner in Carlisle 12.1716. [CAT.205][StAUL.Cheap MS.5/537]

CARNEGY, JAMES, of Findowry, Brechin, Lord Lieutenant Depute of Angus 1745. [LPR158]

CARNEGIE, JAMES, of Boysack, appointed as Envoy to the States of Switzerland 6.11.1716. [JP232]

CARNEGIE, JAMES, the younger, of Balnamoon, Menmuir, born 1713 eldest son of Alexander Carnegie, Captain of Ogilvy's Regiment 1745, escaped to Sweden 1746, died in Scotland 1791.[P2.100] [OR2][GK111]

CARNEGIE, JAMES, of Balmachie, Panbride, Ensign of Ogilvy's Regiment 1745, prisoner in Dundee 1746. [LPR351][OR6]

CARNEGIE, JAMES, surgeon in Brechin, Surgeon in Ogilvy's Regiment 1745. [OR7][LPR158]

CARNEGY, JAMES, a mason in Brechin, soldier of Ogilvy's Regiment 1745. [OR16]

CARNEGY, ROBERT, weaver in Brechin, soldier of Ogilvy's Regiment 1745.[OR16]

CARRIE, JOHN, a pedlar in Arbroath, transported from Liverpool to Virginia on the Gildart 24.2.1747, arrived in Port North Potomac, Maryland, 5.8.1747.   [P.2.102][PRO.T1.28]

CARRIE, THOMAS, weaver in Cotton of Affleck, Monikie, soldier of Ogilvy's Regiment 1745. [OR16]

CATTENACH, JOHN, servant to William Ogilvy in Meikle Kenny, Kingoldrum,soldier of Ogilvy's Regiment 1745, prisoner after Culloden. [OR16]

CATTENACH, JOHN, born 1727, son of Alexander Cattenach, ploughman in Kenny, Kingoldrum, soldier of Ogilvy's Regiment 1745. [OR17]

CAWTY, DAVID, writer and ex Baillie of Forfar, soldier of Ogilvy's Regiment 1745, prisoner at Culloden 1746. [OR19][P2.106]

CHALMERS, ANDREW, ploughman in Glamis, soldier of Ogilvy's Regiment 1745. [OR17]

CHALMERS, FRANCIS, soldier of Ogilvy's Regiment 1745. [OR17]

CHALMERS, JOHN, ploughman in Kinnell Mill, soldier of Ogilvy's Regiment 1745. [OR17]

CHALMERS, JOHN, in Drunkendub, St Vigeans, soldier of Ogilvy's Regiment 1745. [OR17]

CHAPLAIN, JAMES, workman in Arnboggie, Lintrathen, soldier of Ogilvy's Regiment 1745. [OR17]

CHRISTIE, ALEXANDER, servant to Baillie Cawty in Forfar, soldier of Ogilvy's Regiment 1745. [OR17]

CHRISTIE, JAMES, in Kirkton of Auchterhouse, soldier of Ogilvy's Regiment 1745.[OR17]

CHRISTIE, JOHN, born 1694, from Angus, soldier in Ogilvy's Regiment 1745, prisoner in Inverness and Tilbury 1746. [P2.114]

CHRISTIE, PETER, ploughman in Lindertis, Airlie, soldier of Ogilvy's Regiment 1745. [OR17]

CLARK, ALEXANDER, ploughman in Newton of Glamis, soldier of Ogilvy's Regiment 1745. [OR17]

CLARK, ALEXANDER, workman in Braes of Auldallan, Lintrathen, soldier of Ogilvy's Regiment 1745. [OR17]

CLARK, CHARLES, workman in Bank, Kirriemuir, soldier in Ogilvy's Regiment 1745. [OR18]

CLARK, DAVID, workman in Strone, Tannadice, soldier in Ogilvy's Regiment 1745. [OR18]

CLARK, JAMES, servant to James Wright in Berie, Lintrathen, soldier of Ogilvy's Regiment 1745. [OR18]

CLARK, JAMES, sailor in Greenlawhill, Barry, soldier in Ogilvy's Regiment 1745, prisoner at Culloden and Montrose 1746-1747. [OR18][P2.116]

CLARK, JAMES, in Dundee, soldier of Ogilvy's Regiment 1745, prisoner in Arbroath and Montrose 1746-1747, escaped. [P2.116]

CLARK, JOHN, ploughman in Thornton, Glamis, soldier of Ogilvy's Regiment 1745. [OR18]

COCHRANE, DAVID, workman in Kirriemuir, soldier of Ogilvy's Regiment 1745. [OR18]

COLVILL, WILLIAM, son of the laird of Kincardin, Lieutenant of Panmure's regiment, 1715. [SRO.GD45.1.201]

CONSTABLE, JOHN, wright in Dundee, soldier of Ogilvy's Regiment 1745.[OR18]

COOK, JOHN, workman in Dundee, soldier of Ogilvy's Regiment 1745, a prisoner.[OR18]

COPINS, DAVID, workman in Barnton, Kingoldrum, soldier of Ogilvy's Regiment, prisoner in Carlisle. [OR18]

CORNALL, ANDREW, born 1723, crofter in Carseburn, Forfar, soldier in Ogilvy's Regiment 1745, prisoner in Inverness 1746. [OR18][P2.128]

COSKIE, JOHN, in Binaves, Kinnell, soldier of Ogilvy's Regiment
1745.[OR18]
COUPER, GILBERT, Grenadier Lieutenant of Panmure's Foot, 1715.
[SRO.GD45.1.201]
COUTTS, JAMES, mason in Arbroath, soldier of Ogilvy's Regiment 1745,
prisoner 1746-1747. [P2.130]
COWIE, DAVID, in Rossie, Craig, soldier of Ogilvy's Regiment 1745.
[OR18]
COWIE, JOHN, soldier of Ogilvy's Regiment, 1745, prisoner. [OR18]
COWIE, WILLIAM, baker in Montrose, prisoner in Montrose and Stirling
1746.[P2.130]
COWPAR, JOHN, blacksmith in Arbroath, soldier of Ogilvy's Regiment
1745. [OR19]
CRABB, DAVID, born 1698, son of John Crabb in Rescobie, soldier of
Roy Stuart's Regiment, prisoner in Inverness and Tilbury 1746.
[P2.132]
CRAIG, JOHN, town officer of Forfar, prisoner in Forfar and Montrose
1746.[P2.132]
CRAIK, DAVID, in Nether Scythie, Lintrathen, soldier of Ogilvy's
Regiment 1745. [OR19]
CRAIK, JOHN, workman in Upper Scythie, Lintrathen, soldier of Ogilvy's
Regiment 1745. [OR19]
CRAW, ANDREW, from Dundee, Life Guard 1745, prisoner in Dundee
1746-1747. [P2.132]
CRIGHTON, ALEXANDER, workman in Dundee, soldier of Ogilvy's
Regiment, 1745, a prisoner in Dundee 1746-1747. [OR19][P2.134]
CRIGHTON, ALEXANDER, porter in Dundee, soldier of Ogilvy's
Regiment 1745.[OR19]
CRICHTON, DAVID, from Dundee, prisoner in Stirling and Carlisle,
transported 21.3.1747. [P2.134]
CRICHTON, JAMES, shoemaker in Arbroath, soldier of Ogilvy's
Regiment 1745, transported from Liverpool to Virginia on the
Gildart 24.2.1747, landed at Port North Potomac, Maryland,
5.8.1747. [P2.134][PRO.T1.328][OR19]
CRIGHTON, JOHN, servant to Thomas Adam of Cheatley, Lintrathen,
soldier of Ogilvy's Regiment 1745. [OR19]
CRIGHTON, JOHN, ploughman in Cardean, Airlie, soldier of Ogilvy's
Regiment 1745. [OR19]
CRICHTON, JOHN, sailor in Dundee, soldier of Ogilvy's Regiment 1745.
[OR19]
CRICHTON, THOMAS, son of the laird of Ruthven, Lieutenant of
Ogilvy's Regiment 1745. [OR4]

CRICHTON, THOMAS, surgeon in Dundee, Surgeon of Ogilvy's Regiment 1745. [OR7]

CRICHTON, THOMAS, in Brulzeon, Lintrathe, soldier of Ogilvy's Regiment 1745. [OR19]

CRIGHTON, THOMAS, mason in Arbroath, soldier of Ogilvy's Regiment 1745.[OR20]

CRICHTON, THOMAS, ploughman in Glamis, soldier of Ogilvy's Regiment 1745.[OR20]

CRICHTON, WILLIAM, Captain of Panmure's Foot, 1715, taken prisoner at Sheriffmuir. [SRO.GD45.1.201][CAT.205]; in Brussels 1718. [SRO.GD45.14.219.12]

CROCKAT, JAMES, workman in Kingoldrum, soldier of Ogilvy's Regiment 1745.[OR20]

CROW, ANDREW, mason in Dundee, soldier of Ogilvy's Regiment 1745, prisoner in Dundee 1746-1747. [P2.138]

CROW, JAMES, mason in Dundee, soldier of Ogilvy's Regiment 1745, prisoner in Dundee 1746-1747. [OR20][P2.138]

CUMMING, DAVID, in Eassie, soldier of Ogilvy's Regiment 1745. [OR20]

CUMMING, JOHN, Excise surveyor in Montrose, prisoner in Montrose 1746.[P2.140]

CUTHBERT, ARCHIBALD, ploughman in Balnamoon, Menmuir, soldier of Ogilvy's Regiment 1745. [OR20]

DAKERS, GEORGE, in Montrose, Drummer of Ogilvy's Regiment 1745, prisoner in Montrose 1746. [OR8][LPR320]

DALGAIRNS, ALEXANDER, ploughman in Glamis, soldier of Ogilvy's Regiment 1745. [OR20]

DALGLISH, JAMES, labourer in Dundee, soldier of Ogilvy's Regiment 1745. [OR20]

DALL, Mr ROBERT, Lieutenant of Panmure's Foot, 1715. [SRO.GD45.1.201]

DAVIDSON, JAMES, deserter from the Scots Fusiliers, soldier of Lord John Drummond's Regiment, prisoner in Perth and Montrose 1746. [P2.146]

DAVIDSON, JOHN, servant in Brechin,soldier of Ogilvy's Regiment 1745.[OR20]

DAVIDSON, WILLIAM, silversmith in Dundee, soldier of Ogilvy's Regiment 1745, a prisoner in Dundee 1746. [OR20][P2.146]

DAVIE, JOHN, minister in Strathcathro and factor to the Earl of Southesk, deposed 1716. [F.3.418][SRO.CH2.575.1]

DAVIE, JOHN, servant in Dodivoe, Shawfield, Kirriemuir, soldier of Ogilvy's Regiment 1745, a prisoner in Carlisle. [OR21][P2.146]

DEANNIES, DAVID, "a young man" in Binaves, Kinnell, soldier of
Ogilvy's Regiment 1745. [OR21][LPR160]

DEAR, WILLIAM, a meal monger in Brechin, 1745. [LPR162]

DEASE, JAMES, born 1715, merchant in Brechin, 1745, a prisoner in
Inverness and in Tilbury 1746.. [LPR162][P2.146]

DEUCHARS, JOHN, ploughman in Glen Ogilvy, soldier of Ogilvy's
Regiment 1745. [OR21]

DOCTOR, PETER, born 1722, son of Patrick Doctor, ploughman in Glen
Ogilvy, soldier of Ogilvy's Regiment 1745.[OR21]

DOIG, JOHN, born 1722, weaver or crofter in Carseburn, Forfar, soldier
of Ogilvy's Regiment 1745, prisoner in Inverness and at Tilbury.
[OR21][P2.156]

DONALD, JAMES, in Glen Isla, prisoner in Glen Isla 1746. [P2.146]

DONALD, JOHN, servant to Alexander Farquharson in Inzion, Lintrathen,
soldier of Ogilvy's Regiment 1745. [OR21]

DONALDSON, JOHN, carter in Montrose, prisoner in Montrose and
Stirling 1746.[P2.158]

DONALDSON, JOHN, gardener in Ballinloan, Angus, soldier of Roy
Stuart's Regiment 1745, prisoner in England 1746. [P2.158]

DORWARD, DAVID, land labourer in Arbroath, soldier of Ogilvy's
Regiment 1745. [OR21]

DORWARD, DAVID, weaver in Arbroath, soldier of Ogilvy's Regiment
1745. [OR21]

DORMAN, DAVID, burgess of Arbroath, prisoner in Arbroath 1746.
[P2.158]

DOUGLAS, PATRICK, Ensign of Strathmore's Battalion, prisoner in
Preston 1715. [CS.V.162]

DOWNIE, EBENEZER, ploughman in Blackhill, Airlie, soldier of
Ogilvy's Regiment 1745. [OR21]

DUFF, ALEXANDER, apprentice in Dundee, soldier of Ogilvy's
Regiment 1745. [OR21]

DUNCAN, ALEXANDER, of Ardownie, Captain of Panmure's Foot,
1715. [SRO.GD45.1.201]

DUNCAN, ALEXANDER, tacksman of the Customs in Arbroath, soldier
of Ogilvy's Regiment 1745, a prisoner. [OR22]

DUNCAN, CHARLES, workman in Haugh, Kirriemuir, soldier of Ogilvy's
Regiment 1745. [OR22]

DUNCAN, JAMES, brother of Ardownie, Grenadier Lieutenant of
Panmure's Foot 1715. [SRO.GD45.1.201]

DUNCAN, JAMES, workman in Balnaboth, Kirriemuir, soldier of
Ogilvy's Regiment 1745. [OR22]

DUNCAN, JAMES, workman in Crowmuir, Kirriemuir, soldier of
Ogilvy's Regiment 1745. [OR22]

DUNCAN, JOHN, servant to Thomas Hanton in Easter Coull, Lintrathen,
soldier of Ogilvy's Regiment 1745. [OR22]

DUNCAN, JOHN, born 1704, fisherman in Montrose, drummer of
Ogilvy's Regiment 1745, prisoner in Carlisle and York 1746, t
transported from   Liverpool to Virginia on the Gildart 24.2.1747,
landed at Port North Potomac, Maryland, 5.8.1747.
[PRO.T1.328][P2.170]

DUNCAN, JOHN, born 1698, merchant and stampmaster of Brechin,
1745, prisoner in Inverness and Tilbury, pardoned on enlistment.
[LPR162][P2.172]

DUNCAN, JOHN, brewer in Arbroath, soldier of Ogilvy's Regiment 1745.
[OR22]

DUNCAN, JOHN, born 1731, apprentice carpenter in Dundee, soldier of
Ogilvy's Regiment 1745, prisoner in Carlisle and York 1746,
transported 1747. [P2.172][OR22]

DUNCAN, PETER, born 1714, workman in Dundee, soldier of Ogilvy's
Regiment 1745, prisoner in Canongate and Carlisle 1746,
transported from Liverpool to Virginia on the Gildart 24.2.1747,
landed at Port North Potomac,Maryland, 5.8.1747.
[OR22][P2.172][PRO.T1.328]

DUNCAN, ROBERT, farmer in Milton of Glen Esk, soldier of Ogilvy's
Regiment 1745. [OR22]

DUTHIE, ALEXANDER, born 1722, son of George Duthie and Katherine
Steel, smith in Brechin, 1745. [LPR162]

DUTHIE, JOHN, born 1726, son of David Duthie, weaver in Hirdhill,
Kirriemuir,   soldier of Ogilvy's Regiment 1745, a prisoner in
Carlisle 1745. [OR22][P2.172]

DUTHIE, JOHN, ploughman in Newton of Airlie, soldier of Ogilvy's
Regiment 1745.   [OR22]

EASSIE, JOHN, labourer in Braidstone, Airlie, soldier of Ogilvy's
Regiment 1745.[OR23]

EASSON, ANDREW, workman in Newmill, Lintrathen, soldier of
Ogilvy's Regiment 1745. [OR23]

EDGAR, JAMES, of Keithock, born 13.7.1688 younger son of David
Edgar of Keithock and Elizabeth Guthrie, Secretary to the Chevalier
de St George, appointed Clerk of the Council, died 24.9.1764.
[HHA173][JP.249]

EDGAR, JOHN, son of Alexander Edgar and Margaret Skinner, Life
Guard in 1745, fled to America, captured by a French privateer,
taken to France, commissioned in Ogilvy's Regiment there, died in
Scotland 4.4.1788. [JP249]

EDGAR, ROBERT, Keithock, out in 1715, merchant in Montrose,
prisoner in Montrose and Stirling 1746, died in Stirling Castle{?}.
[JP249][P2.176]

EDWARD, ALEXANDER, labourer in Hillockhead, Lintrathen. soldier of
Ogilvy's Regiment, 1745. [OR23]

EDWARD, ALEXANDER, workman in Kingoldrum, soldier of Ogilvy's
Regiment 1745, killed. [OR23][LPR208]

EDWARD, ANDREW, born 25.4.1722 son of Alexander Edward in
Kirriemuir, servant to William Grewar in Purgavie, Lintrathen,
soldier of Ogilvy's Regiment 1745, prisoner in Carlisle and York
1746, transported from Liverpool to the Leeward Islands on the
Veteran 5.5.1747, liberated and landed on Martinique 6.1747.
[OR23][P2.176][PRO.SP36.102]

EDWARD, ANDREW, workman in Newbigging, Lintrathen, soldier of
Ogilvy's Regiment 1745.[OR23]

EDWARD, ANDREW, chapman in Braes, Lintrathen, soldier of Ogilvy's
Regiment 1745. [OR2]

EDWARD, DAVID, workman in Boghead of Lednathie, Kirriemuir,
soldier of Ogilvy's Regiment 1745. [OR23]

EDWARD, JAMES, workman in Pearsie, Kirriemuir, soldier of Ogilvy's
Regiment 1745. [OR23]

EDWARD, JAMES, son of Alexander Edward, in West Reverney,
Lintrathen, soldier of Ogilvy's Regiment 1745, prisoner in Stirling
Castle 1746, transported 1747. [OR23][P.2.176]

EDWARD, JAMES, in Ferryden, soldier of Ogilvy's Regiment 1745.
[OR24]

EDWARD, JOHN, workman in Netherton, Kirriemuir, soldier of Ogilvy's
Regiment 1745. [OR24]

EDWARD, JOHN, farmer in Needs, Lintrathen, soldier of Ogilvy's
Regiment 1745.[OR24]

EDWARD, JOHN, workman in Bottom. Lintrathen, soldier of Ogilvy's
Regiment 1745. [OR24]

EDWARD, JOHN, in Greenlamirth, Lintrathen, soldier of Ogilvy's
Regiment 1745. [OR24]

EDWARD, JOHN, in Glen Isla, soldier of Ogilvy's Regiment 1745,
prisoner in Dundee 1746. [P2.176]

ELLIS, ALEXANDER, labourer in Glen Ogilvy, soldier of Ogilvy's
Regiment 1745.[OR24]

ELLIS, JOHN, labourer in Cardean, Airlie, soldier of Ogilvy's Regiment 1745. [OR24]

ERSKINE, ALEXANDER, in Montrose, prisoner in Montrose and Stirling Castle 1746. [P2.178]

ERSKINE, FRANCIS, son of the laird of Kirkbuddo, Lieutenant of Panmure's Foot, 1715. [SRO.GD45.1.201][cf ...Erskine, an Ensign who was courtmartialled and shot 1715 - CS.V.175]

ERSKINE. JOHN, an apprentice merchant in Montrose, Ensign of Ogilvy's Regiment 1745. [OR6][LPR.162/321]

ESSIE, JAMES, sr., weaver in Arbroath, soldier of Ogilvy's Regiment 1745. [OR24]

FAIRWEATHER, PETER, a baker's servant in Brechin, soldier of Ogilvy's Regiment 1745. [OR24]

FALCONER, JOHN, soldier of Ogilvy's Regiment 1745. [OR24]

FARQUHAR, DAVID, labourer in Lindertis, Kirriemuir, soldier of Ogilvy's Regiment 1745. [OR24]

FARQUHARSON, ALEXANDER, farmer in Inzeon, Lintrathen, Lieutenant of Ogilvy's Regiment 1745. [OR4]

FARQUHARSON, ALEXANDER, workman in East Reverney, Lintrathen, soldier of Ogilvy's Regiment 1745. [OR25]

FARQUHARSON, JAMES, farmer's son in Westertown, Lintrathen, soldier of Ogilvy's Regiment 1745. [OR25]

FARQUHARSON, JOHN, farmer in Over Scythy, Lintrathen, Lieutenant of Ogilvy's Regiment 1745. [OR4]

FARQUHARSON, WILLIAM, of Broughdearg, Glen Isla, a farmer, Captain of Ogilvy's Regiment 1745. [OR2]

FARQUHARSON, WILLIAM, workman in West Coull, Lintrathen, soldier of Ogilvy's Regiment 1745. [OR25]

FEITHIE, ANDREW, labourer in Lindertis, Kirriemuir, soldier of Ogilvy's Regiment 1745, hanged at Forfar 11.9.1746. [OR25]

FEITHIE, JOHN, workman in Kirriemuir, soldier of Ogilvy's Regiment 1745. [OR25]

FENTON, DAVID, farmer in Little Kenny, Kingoldrum, Lieutenant of Ogilvy's Regiment 1745. [OR4]

FENTON, JAMES, workman in Kinclune, Kingoldrum, soldier of Ogilvy's Regiment 1745. [OR25]

FENTON, JOHN, farmer in Purgavie, Lintrathen, soldier of Ogilvy's Regiment 1745, died in 1789. [OR25]

FENTON, SYLVESTER, labourer in Linross, Airlie, soldier of Ogilvy's Regiment 1745. [OR25]

FENTON, THOMAS, servant in Dundee, soldier of Ogilvy's Regiment 1745.[OR25]

FERGUSON, JOSEPH, labourer in Braideston, Airlie, soldier of Ogilvy's
Regiment 1745. [OR25]

FERGUSON, JOSEPH, weaver in Chapel of Keillor, Dundee, soldier of
Ogilvy's Regiment 1745. [OR26]

FERGUSON, ROBERT, threadmaker in Dundee, soldier of Ogilvy's
Regiment 1745, prisoner in Dundee 1746-1747.[P2.190][OR26]

FERGUSON, WILLIAM, Excise Officer in Arbroath, 1745, prisoner in
Arbroath and Montrose 1746. [LPR164][P2.190]

FERRIER, DAVID, of Unthank, merchant and farmer in Brechin, Captain
of Ogilvy's Regiment 1745, Depute Governor of Brechin, escaped
to Spain.   [OR2][LPR164]

FERRIER, JOHN, in Cotton of Carcary, Farnell, soldier of Ogilvy's
Regiment 1745, a prisoner in Lethnot and Montrose 1746.
[OR26][P2.190]

FERRIER, JOHN, born 1710, fishmonger in Little Carcary, soldier of
Ogilvy's Regiment 1745, prisoner in Inverness and Tilbury 1746.
[P2.190]

FERRIER, ROBERT, a farmer in Arbroath, Ensign of Ogilvy's Regiment
1745. [OR6]

FETTES, DAVID, born 1728, servant in West Fithie, Farnell, soldier of
Ogilvy's Regiment 1745, prisoner in Inverness and Tilbury 1746,
transported 31.3.1747 from London to Barbados in the
Frere.[P2.192][OR26]

FETTES, JOHN, maltman in Montrose, soldier of Ogilvy's Regiment
1745, prisoner in Montrose 1746. [OR26][LPR320]

FIFE, ..., schoolmaster and session clerk of Arbroath, deposed 3.1716.
[SRO.CH2.15.3]

FILP, THOMAS, sr., labourer in Thornton, Glamis, soldier of Ogilvy's
Regiment 1745. [OR26]

FILP, THOMAS, jr., labourer in Lindertis, Airlie, soldier of Ogilvy's
Regiment 1745. [OR26]

FINDLAY, FRANCIS, in Cortachy, soldier of Ogilvy's Regiment 1745.
[OR26]

FINDLAY, JAMES, workman in Meams, Kirriemuir, soldier of Ogilvy's
Regiment 1745. [OR26]

FINDLAY, JAMES, workman in Bruntyleave, Kirriemuir, soldier of
Ogilvy's Regiment 1745. [OR26]

FLETCHER, ROBERT, the younger, of Ballinshoe, Kirriemuir, Major of
Ogilvy's Regiment, escaped from Dundee via Bergen and Sweden to
France 1746. [OR1/127][LPR210][GK113]

FODD, WILLIAM, born 1692, son of Andrew Fodd, crofter in
Carseburn, Forfar, soldier of Ogilvy's Regiment 1745, prisoner in
Inverness and Tilbury 1746. [OR26][P2.218]

FORBES, ALEXANDER, servant to James Craik in Bridgend, Lintrathen,
soldier of Ogilvy's Regiment 1745, drowned. [OR26]

FORDUE, JAMES, wright in Arbroath, 1745. [LPR164]

FORRESTER, SYLVESTER, born 1713, son of John Forrester, workman
in Ley, Lintrathen, soldier of Ogilvy's Regiment 1745. [OR27]

FORRESTER, WILLIAM, born 1720, son of John Forrester, workman in
Kinclune, Kingoldrum, soldier of Ogilvy's Regiment 1745. [OR27]

FOTHERINGHAM, ARCHIBALD, son of the laird of Powrie, Lieutenant
of Panmure's Foot, 1715, fought at Sheriffmuir, a prisoner in
Carlisle 12.1716. [SRO.GD45.1.201][CAT.205][StAUL.Cheap
MS.5/537]

FOTHERINGHAM, DAVID, merchant in Dundee, Governor of Dundee
1745, escaped from Dundee via Bergen to Sweden 5.1746.
[OR127] [GK113]

FOTHERINGHAM, DAVID, born 1708, a merchant, prisoner in Tilbury
8.1746.[P2.206]

FOTHERINGHAM, JAMES, born 1717, son of George Fotheringham and
Janet White, fishmonger in Upper Tenements of Caldhame, Brechin,
soldier of Ogilvy's Regiment 1745. [OR27][LPR166]

FOTHERINGHAM, JOHN, transported from Liverpool to South Carolina
on the Susanna 7.5.1716. [SPC.1716.309][CTB.31.206]

FOTHERINGHAM, THOMAS, of Bandeen, Officer of the Life Guards,
escaped to Sweden 1746. [GK113]

FRASER, HUGH, blacksmith in Montrose, soldier of Ogilvy's Regiment
1745, a prisoner in Montrose 1746. [OR27][LPR320]

FRASER, JOHN, maltman in Kirriemuir, soldier of Ogilvy's Regiment
1745. [OR27]

FRASER, JOHN, lodger in Paddocksmire, Kinnell, soldier of Ogilvy's
Regiment 1745. [OR27]

FRASER, JOHN, servant in Rossie, Craig, soldier of Ogilvy's Regiment
1745.[OR27]

FRIZEL, JOHN, mason in Upper Tenements of Caldhame, Brechin,
soldier of Ogilvy's Regiment 1745. [OR27]

FULLERTON, ALEXANDER, farmer in Edzell, Captain of Ogilvy's
Regiment 1745, prisoner in Montrose, Stirling, and Edinburgh
1746.[P2.218]

FULLERTON, HENRY, farmer, prisoner in Stirling 1746. [P2.220]

FULLERTON, JOHN, merchant in Montrose, prisoner in Montrose and
Stirling 1746.[P2.220]

FYFE, JAMES, servant in Forfar, soldier of Ogilvy's Regiment 1745.
[OR27]

GAMMACK, WILLIAM, clerk in Glamis, 1745. [LPR214]

GARDINER, ANDREW, weaver in Dundee, prisoner in Arbroath and
Canongate 1746. [P2.220]

GARDYNE, [Gairn?], CHARLES, Lieutenant of Panmure's Foot, 1715.
[SRO.GD45.1.201]

GARDYNE, [Gairn?], CHARLES, Adjutant of Panmure's Foot, 1715.
[SRO.GD45.1.201]

GARDYNE, [Gairn?], DAVID, of Lawtoun, Captain of Panmure's Foot,
1715, taken prisoner at Sheriffmuir.[SRO.GD45.1.201][CAT.205]

GARDYNE, DAVID, the younger, of Lawtoun, Inverkeilor, Captain of
Ogilvy's Regiment 1745, escaped to via Sweden to Flanders.
[OR2][LPR168][GK113]

GEDDIE, ANDREW, minister of Farnell, died before 2.1719. [F.3.393]

GEIGIE, GEORGE, weaver in Dundee, soldier of Ogilvy's Regiment
1745.[OR27]

GELLATLY, JAMES, brewer's servant, Liff, soldier of Ogilvy's Regiment
1745.[OR28]

GIBB, JAMES, sailor in Dundee, soldier of Ogilvy's Regiment 1745.
[OR28]

GIBSON, DAVID, porter in Dundee, soldier of Ogilvy's Regiment
1745.[OR27]

GIBSON, JAMES, in Farnell, soldier of Ogilvy's Regiment 1745, escaped
to Russia. [OR27]

GIBSON, JOHN, chapman in Caldhame, Brechin, soldier of Ogilvy's
Regiment 1745.[OR27]

GIBSON, JOHN, in Cotton of Affleck, Monikie, soldier of Ogilvy's
Regiment 1745.[OR27]

GIBSON, JOHN, born 1727, weaver in Dundee, soldier of Ogilvy's
Regiment 1745, transported from Liverpool to Virginia on the
Gildart, arrived in Port North Potomac, Maryland, 5.8.1747.
[OR27][P.2.228][PRO.T1.328]

GILLESPIE, WILLIAM, born 1721 son of William Gillespie and Janet
Mitchell, sailor in Arbroath, 1745, prisoner in Arbroath 1746.
[LPR168][P2.228]

GLENDAY, JAMES, born 1720 son of James Glenday, grieve in Reedie,
Airlie, soldier of Ogilvy's Regiment 1745. [OR27]

GLENDAY, JOHN, transported from Liverpool to Virginia on the
Friendship 24.5.1716, landed in Maryland 8.1716.
[SPC.1716.311][HM.386]

GLENDAY, JOHN, weaver in Denhead of Logie, Kirriemuir, soldier of Ogilvy's Regiment 1745. [OR27]

GOLD, PATRICK, Ensign of Panmure's Foot, 1715. [SRO.GD45.1.201]

GORDON, JOHN, jr., barber in Forfar, soldier of Ogilvy's Regiment 1745. [OR28]

GORDON, JOHN, apprentice surgeon in Montrose, soldier of Ogilvy's Regiment 1745, prisoner in Montrose 1746. [OR29][LPR320]

GORDON, PATRICK, Lieutenant of Panmure's Foot, 1715. [SRO.GD45.1.201]

GORDON, WILLIAM, apprentice writer in Montrose, soldier of Ogilvy's Regiment 1745, prisoner in Montrose 1746.[OR29][LPR320]

GOUCK, DAVID, born 16.6.1723, son of John Gouck and Margaret Comb in Farnell, a servant in Egypt, Farnell, soldier of Ogilvy's Regiment 1745, transported from Liverpool to Barbados on the Frere 31.3.1747. [OR29][P.2.232]

GOURLAY, GEORGE, born 1722 son of Alexander Gourlay and Margaret Thain, in Panbride, soldier of Ogilvy's Regiment 1745. [OR29]

GOURLAY, JAMES, born 1715, son of Alexander Gourlay and Margaret Thain, in Panbride, soldier of Ogilvy's Regiment 1745. [OR29]

GOW, DONALD, workman in Pitewan, Lintrathen, soldier of Ogilvy's Regiment 1745. [OR29]

GOWANS, WILLIAM, ploughman in Mill of Kinnell, soldier of Ogilvy's Regiment 1745. [OR29]

GRAHAM. ALEXANDER, merchant in Dundee, escaped to Sweden 1746. [GK114]

GRAHAM, ALEXANDER, writer in Dundee, Life Guard 1745. [LPR214]

GRAHAM, DAVID, merchant in Dundee, Life Guard 1745, prisoner in Dundee 1746. [LPR214/351]

GRAHAM, JAMES, of Duntroon, Life Guard 1745. [LPR214]

GRAHAM, JAMES, of Duntroon, son of William Graham and Christina Graham, Viscount Dundee, Life Guard 1745, escaped from Dundee via Bergen to Sweden 1746, later to France, died in Dunkirk 1759. [GK114][OR127]

GRANT, JAMES, brewer in Arbroath, soldier of Ogilvy's Regiment 1745. [OR29]

GRANT, PATRICK, farmer in Shielhill, Kirriemuir, Captain of Ogilvy's Regiment 1745. [OR2][LPR214]

GRANT, WILLIAM, weaver in Auldbar, soldier of Ogilvy's Regiment 1745, prisoner in Dundee and Canongate 1746. [P2.264]

GRANT, WILLIAM, in Brechin, soldier of Ogilvy's Regiment 1745, prisoner in Montrose and Edinburgh 1746. [P2.264]

GRAY, ANDREW, weaver in Glamis, soldier of Ogilvy's Regiment 1745. [OR29]

GRAY, DAVID, servant in Dundee, soldier of Ogilvy's Regiment 1745. [OR29]

GRAY, DAVID, brewer in Arbroath, soldier of Ogilvy's Regiment 1745. [OR29]

GRAY, DAVID, weaver in Arbroath, prisoner in Arbroath and London 1746. [P2.266]

GRAY, JAMES, cottar in Cotton of Gowanhead, Kinnell, soldier of Ogilvy's Regiment 1745. [OR29]

GRAY, JOHN, born 1724, weaver in Brankin, Liff, soldier of Ogilvy's Regiment 1745, prisoner in Perth and Carlisle 1746, transported from Liverpool to Virginia on the Johnson, landed at Port Oxford, Maryland, 5.8.1747. [OR30][P2.266][PRO.T1.328]

GRAY, JOHN, weaver, soldier of Ogilvy's Regiment 1745, prisoner in Perth and in the Canongate 1746-1747. [P2.166]

GRAY, WILLIAM, painter in Montrose, soldier of Ogilvy's Regiment 1745.[OR30]

GRAY, WILLIAM, from Brechin, apprentice surgeon in Perth, surgeon's mate 1745, prisoner in Edinburgh 1746-1748, pardoned on enlistment 1748.[P2.268]

GREENHILL, ROBERT, grieve in Brighton, Kinnettles, Sergeant of Ogilvy's Regiment, 1745. [OR9]

GREGORIE, JOHN, Ensign of Panmure's Foot, 1715. [SRO.GD45.1.201]

GREGORIE, MALCOLM, "one of Aboyne's men", Captain of Panmure's Foot, 1715. [SRO.GD45.1.201]

GREIG, ALEXANDER, merchant in Dysart, Maryton, soldier of Ogilvy's Regiment 1745. [OR30]

GREIG, ALEXANDER, jr., merchant in Dysart, Maryton, soldier of Ogilvy's Regiment 1745. [OR30][LPR320]

GREIG, JAMES, farmer in Woodhill, Barry, soldier of Ogilvy's Regiment 1746, prisoner at Culloden and in Arbroath [OR30][LPR212][P2.268]

GREWER, GEORGE, labourer in Glen Isla, soldier of Ogilvy's Regiment 1745, transported from Liverpool 22.4.1747.[P.2.268]

GREWER, WILLIAM, servant to Alexander Farquharson in Cordauch, Lintrathen, soldier of Ogilvy's Regiment 1745. [OR30]

GRUB, DAVID, carter in Montrose, prisoner in Stirling Castle 1746. [P2.270]

GRUB, JAMES, Episcopalian preacher in Carmyllie ca.1715. [HHA.170]

GRUB, JAMES, in Cortachy, prisoner in Stirling Castle 1746-1747.
[P2.270]

GUILD, THOMAS, born 1687 son of Thomas Guild, in Glamis,
transported from Liverpool to South Carolina on the Susanna,
7.5.1716, a planter in Colleton County, South Carolina, probate
1737 South Carolina. [SPC.1716.309][CTB.31.206]

GUTHRIE, ALEXANDER, an Episcopal preacher in Arbroath ca.1715.
[HHA.170]

GUTHRIE, GEORGE, in Montrose, soldier of Ogilvy's Regiment 1745,
prisoner in Montrose 1746. [OR30][LPR320]

GUTHRIE, GIDEON, an Episcopal preacher in Brechin, deposed 1716.
[SRO.CH2.575.1]

GUTHRIE, JOHN, transported from Liverpool to South Carolina on th
Susanna 7.5.1716. [SPC.1716.309][CTB.31.206]

GUTHRIE, JOHN, transported from Liverpool to South Carolina on the
Wakefield 21.5.1716. [CTB.31.205]

GUTHRIE, ROBERT, transported from Liverpool to South Carolina on
the Wakefield 21.4.1716. [SPC.1716.309][CTB.31.205]

GUTHRIE, ROBERT, merchant in Dundee, 1745, prisoner in Dundee.
[LPR214]

HACKIE, JOHN, weaver in Dundee, soldier of Ogilvy's Regiment
1745.[OR30]

HALIBURTON, THOMAS, wright in Dundee, soldier of Ogilvy's
Regiment 1745. [OR30]

HAY, GEORGE, in Montrose, soldier of Ogilvy's Regiment 1745,
prisoner in Montrose 1746. [OR30][LPR320]

HENDERSON, ALEXANDER, merchant in Dundee, 1745. [LPR216]

HENDERSON, CHARLES, servant in Rescobie, soldier of Ogilvy's
Regiment 1745, killed. [OR30]

HENDERSON, FRANCIS, merchant in Dundee, 1745, prisoner in
Dundee. [LPR216]

HENDERSON, JAMES, born 1717, a cook, prisoner in Carlisle and
Lancaster,   transported from Liverpool on the Veteran to the
Leeward Islands, liberated and landed on Martinique 6.1747.
[P.2.282][OR31][PRO.SP36.102]

HENDERSON, JAMES, skipper in Montrose, 1745, prisoner in Montrose
1746-1747. [LPR172/320][P2.284]

HENDERSON, JAMES, slater in Dundee, soldier of Ogilvy's Regiment
1745. [OR31]

HENDERSON, JAMES, servant in Forfar, soldier of Ogilvy's Regiment
1745. [OR31]

HENDERSON, ROBERT, cottar in Cotton of Kinblethmont, Inverkeillor, soldier of Ogilvy's Regiment 1745. [OR31]

HENDERSON, THOMAS, soldier in Ogilvy's Regiment 1745. [OR31]

HENDERSON, WILLIAM, quartermaster of Strathmore's Battalion, a prisoner at Preston 1715, transported to South Carolina or the West Indies 1716. [CS.V.162][CTB.31.205]

HENDERSON, WILLIAM, slater in Dundee, soldier of Ogilvy's Regiment 1745.[OR31]

HENRY, ALEXANDER, dyer in Dundee, soldier of Ogilvy's Regiment 1745.[OR31]

HERSCHELL, DAVID, born 29.10.1699 in Brechin, son of David Herschell and Katherine Adam, a shoemaker in Brechin, soldier of Ogilvy's Regiment 1745, prisoner in Inverness and Tilbury, transported to Jamaica or Barbados 31.3.1747. [P.2.282]

HOBART, JOHN, workman in Nether Shielhill, Kirriemuir, soldier of Ogilvy's Regiment 1745. [OR31]

HODGE, ROBERT, farmer in Fannocksmire, Kinnell, soldier of Ogilvy's Regiment 1745. [OR31]

HOOD, CHARLES, smith in Craigie, prisoner in Dundee 1746-1747. [P2.290]

HOOD, JAMES, jr., blacksmith in Brechin, soldier of Ogilvy's Regiment 1745. [OR31]

HOOD, PATRICK, weaver in Forfar, soldier of Ogilvy's Regiment 1745. [OR31]

HORN, CHARLES, shoemaker in Dundee, Sergeant of Ogilvy's Regiment 1745, prisoner in Dundee 1746. [LPR351] [OR9]

HORN, WILLIAM, born 23.6.1717 in Glamis son of George Horn, a l labourer in Holemill, Glamis, soldier of Ogilvy's Regiment 1745, prisoner in Perth, Canongate, and Carlisle, 1746, transported 1747. [P.2.290][OR32]

HOW, ANDREW, weaver in Burnside of Kirkbuddo, soldier of Ogilvy's Regiment 1745. [OR32]

HUNTER, ADAM, Excise officer in Montrose, 1745, prisoner ther 1746-1747. [LPR170][P2.292]

HUNTER, DAVID, of Burnside, Grange of Monifieth, Captain of Life Guards 1745, escaped from Dundee to Norway, a prisoner in Bergen, later in Sweden 1746. [LPR218][GK114][OR127]

HUNTER, HENRY, born 1717 son of David Hunter and Jean Watt, in Newton of Arbirlot, soldier of Ogilvy's Regiment 1745.[OR32]

HUNTER, JAMES, in Cotton of Letham, St Vigeans, soldier of Ogilvy's Regiment 1745. [OR32]

HUNTER, JAMES, son of John Hunter in Newbigging, St Vigeans, soldier of Ogilvy's Regiment 1745. [OR32]

HUNTER, JOHN, in Newton of Arbirlot, soldier of Ogilvy's Regiment 1745. [OR32]

HUTCHEON, JOHN, weaver in Loanend of Lour, Forfar, soldier of Ogilvy's Regiment 1745. [OR32]

HUTCHISON, ALEXANDER, from Montrose, the Prince's groom, prisoner in Larbert, Stirling, and Carlisle, 1746-1748, pardoned on enlistment. [P2.294]

HUTCHISON, JOHN, a merchant in Arbroath, a prisoner in Edinburgh and in Carlisle 1716, escaped to Bordeaux 1716. [JAB.156] [PRO.SP.54.12.147][CRA.230][SRO.GD45.14.219.6]

HUTCHISON, WILLIAM, labourer in Cossins, Glamis, soldier of Ogilvy's Regiment 1745. [OR32]

INVERARITY, DAVID, meal merchant in Caldhame, Brechin, soldier of Ogilvy's Regiment 1745. [OR32]

INVERARITY, DAVID, shoemaker in Brechin, soldier 1745. [LPR172]

IRONS, ROBERT, in Montrose, soldier of Ogilvy's Regiment 1745, a prisoner in Montrose. [OR32][LPR320]

IRVINE, DAVID, shoemaker in Brechin, soldier of Ogilvy's Regiment 1745. [OR33]

JACKSON, CHARLES, maltman and brewer in Dundee, 1745, a prisoner in Dundee 1746. [LPR218][P2.300]

JACKSON, WILLIAM, born 28.4.1725, son of John Jackson and Elizabeth Fife in Kettins, a labourer, soldier of Ogilvy's Regiment 1745, transported 5.5.1747 from Liverpool to the Leeward Islands on the Veteran, liberated and landed on Martinique 6.1747. [OR33][P.2.300][PRO.SP.36.102]

JAMIESON, WILLIAM, a reedmaker in Montrose, Sergeant of Ogilvy's Regiment 1745, possibly a prisoner in Carlisle and York 1746. [OR9][LPR320][P2.300]

JARROW, JOHN, town officer of Montrose, prisoner in Montrose, Stirling and Edinburgh 1746. [P2.302]

JOHNSTON, ALEXANDER, silversmith in Dundee, Life Guard 1745, escaped from Dundee to Norway 1746, a prisoner in Bergen, later in France. [LPR218][OR127]

JOHNSTON, ALEXANDER, labourer in Glamis, soldier of Ogilvy's Regiment 1745.[OR33]

JOHNSTON, ANDREW, soldier of Ogilvy's Regiment 1745, a prisoner. [OR33]

JOHNSTON, GEORGE, in Balfour, Angus, factor to Lord Panmure, 1745, prisoner in Dundee 1746. [LPR218][P2.304]

JOHNSTON, JAMES, labourer in Balgownie, Eassie, soldier of Ogilvy's Regiment 1745. [OR33]

KEAY, JOHN, tailor in Arbroath, soldier of Ogilvy's Regiment 1745. [OR33]

KEILL, THOMAS, born 1718 son of John Keill and Grizel Eaton, servant to James Ferrier in Kintrochat, Brechin, soldier of Ogilvy's Regiment 1745. [OR33]

KEARSALL, DAVID, from Brechin, soldier of Ogilvy's Regiment 1745, prisoner in Montrose 1746. [P2.308]

KEITH, DAVID, born 1716, farmer in Invercruiven, Montrose, prisoner in Inverness and Tilbury 1746. [P2.308]

KER, HENRY, Ensign in Strathmore's Battalion, a prisoner in Preston 1716. [CS.V.162]

KERMOCK, ANDREW, workman in Craig, Kirriemuir, soldier of Ogilvy's Regiment 1745. [OR33]

KERRIE, ALEXANDER, sailor in Arbroath, soldier of Ogilvy's Regiment 1745, a prisoner. [OR34]

KERRIE, JOHN, merchant in Arbroath, soldier of Ogilvy's Regiment 1745, a prisoner in Edinburgh 1746. [OR34][P2.318]

KERRY, ROBERT, farmer in Newton of Panbride, soldier of Ogilvy's Regiment 1745, prisoner in Arbroath 1746. [OR34][LPR218][P2.102/320]

KIDD, ALEXANDER, transported from Liverpool to Jamaica or Virginia on the Elizabeth and Anne 29.6.1716, landed in Virginia. [SPC.1716.310][CTB.31.208][VSP.1.185]

KIDD, JAMES, precentor and schoolmaster in Arbroath ca.1715. [HHA.171]

KINLOCH, Sir JAMES, of Kinloch, in Dundee, Colonel of Ogilvy's Regiment 1745.[LPR218]

KINLOCH, JOHN, the younger, of Kilry and Logie, Kirriemuir, Captain of Ogilvy's Regiment 1745, escaped to France. [LPR218][OR2]

KINNEAR, PETER, labourer in Glen Ogilvy, soldier of Ogilvy's Regiment 1745. [OR34]

KINNEAR, THOMAS, farmer in Milton of Glen Esk, soldier of Ogilvy's Regiment 1745. [OR34]

KINNIMOND, ALEXANDER, mason in Dundee, prisoner in Dundee 1746. [P2.324]

LACKIE, ALEXANDER, workman in Kingoldrum, soldier of Ogilvy's Regiment 1745. [OR34]

LAING, JOHN, servant in Old Montrose, soldier of Ogilvy's Regiment 1745, killed.[OR34]

LAIRD, ANDREW, merchant in Dundee, prisoner in Dundee 1746.

[LPR222][P2.328]

LAIRD, JOHN, workman in Glamis, soldier of Ogilvy's Regiment 1745.
[OR34]

LAMOND, ALEXANDER, horse hirer in Montrose, prisoner in
Montrose, Stirling and Edinburgh 1746-1747. [O2.330]

LAWRENCE, JAMES, beadle of St Vigean's, deposed 4.1716.
[HHA.170][SRO.CH2.15.3]

LAWSON, JAMES, servant to Sir John Ogilvy in Caldhame, Kirriemuir,
soldier of Ogilvy's Regiment 1745. [OR34]

LAWSON, JAMES, born 1725, workman in Wester Coull, Lintrathen,
soldier of Ogilvy's Regiment 1745, prisoner in Carlisle, transported
from Liverpool on the _Veteran 5.5.1747 to the Leeward Islands,
liberated and landed on Martinique 6.1747.
[P.2.234][OR34][PRO.SP.36.102][LPR220]

LAWSON, JOHN, labourer in Airniefoul, Glamis, soldier of Ogilvy's
Regiment 1745.[OR34]

LAWSON, PETER, miller in Bridgend of Lintrathen, soldier of Ogilvy's
Regiment 1745, prisoner in Blackness. [OR35][LPR220]

LAWSON, THOMAS, ploughman in Woodend, Kirriemuir, soldier of
Ogilvy's Regiment 1745. [OR35]

LEIGHTON, ..., ploughman in Buckhood, Kirriemuir, soldier of
Ogilvy's Regiment 1745. [OR35]

LEITH, JOHN, born 1728, cooper in Brechin, brother of William Leith,
prisoner in Brechin, Montrose, Inverness and Tilbury1746.
[LPR174][P2.338]

LEITH, WILLIAM, in Brechin, Ensign of Ogilvy's Regiment 1745. [OR6]

LESLIE, ALEXANDER, Major of Panmure's Foot, 1715, in Bordeaux by
1719 [SRO.GD45.1.201.21]

LESLIE, WILLIAM, mariner in Montrose, pilot in French service,
prisoner in Berwick-on-Tweed 1746. [LPR174/320][P2.340]

LEUCHARS, JAMES, in Glen Esk, Sergeant of Ogilvy's Regiment 1745.
[OR9]

LINDSAY, HENRY, son of David Lindsay minister in Dunnichen, died
1720. [F.3.282]

LINDSAY, JOHN, of Pitscandly, a prisoner in Carlisle 12.1716.
[StAUL.Cheap MS.5/537]

LINDSAY, JOHN, a surgeon's apprentice in Montrose, Lieutenant of
Ogilvy's Regiment 1745. [OR4][LPR320]

LINDSAY, ROBERT, Episcopal preacher in Edzell, deposed 1716.
[SRO.CH2.575.1]

LINDSAY, WILLIAM, shoemaker in Montrose, soldier of Ogilvy's
Regiment 1745, prisoner in Montrose 1746. [OR35][LPR320]

LITTLEJOHN, ALEXANDER, physician in Montrose, prisoner 1746.
[LPR176]

LITTLEJOHN, DAVID, servant to William Robb in Burghhill, Brechin,
soldier of Ogilvy's Regiment 1745. [OR35][LPR174]

LIVIETH, JOHN, labourer in Haystown, Glamis, soldier of Ogilvy's
Regiment 1745, prisoner in Inverness and Tilbury 1746.
[OR35][P2.346]

LIVIETH, WILLIAM, labourer in Haystown, Glamis, soldier of Ogilvy's
Regiment 1745. [OR35]

LOGIE, PETER, tailor in Tigerton, Menmuir, soldier of Ogilvy's Regiment
1745, prisoner 1746. [P2.346]

LOTHIAN, JOHN, ploughman in Easter Peel, Lintrathen, soldier of
Ogilvy's Regiment 1745. [OR35]

LOVELL, ANDREW, in Panbride, soldier of Ogilvy's Regiment 1745.
[OR35]

LOW, ALEXANDER, merchant in Brechin, 1745, prisoner. [LPR174]

LOW, DAVID, labourer in Glamis, soldier of Ogilvy's Regiment 1745.
[OR35]

LOW, JAMES, servant to James Low in Culhawk, Kirriemuir, soldier of
Ogilvy's Regiment 1745. [OR36]

LOW, JOHN, born 1728, wigmaker in Montrose, soldier of Ogilvy's
Regiment 1745, servant to a French officer, prisoner in Inverness
and Tilbury 1746. [LPR176][P2.350]

LOW, WILLIAM, chapman in Brechin, soldier of Ogilvy's Regiment
1745, prisoner in Dundee 1746. [LPR351][OR36]

LOW, WILLIAM, jr., blacksmith in Montrose, soldier of Ogilvy's
Regiment 1745.[OR36]

LOWPAR, JOHN, blacksmith in Arbroath, soldier of Ogilvy's Regiment
1745. [OR36]

LUMGAIR, JAMES, born 1722 son of John Lumgair and Jean Clark, in
Panbride, soldier of Ogilvy's Regiment 1745. [OR36]

LUNAN, DAVID, weaver in Loanhead of Lour, Forfar, soldier of Ogilvy's
Regiment 1745. [OR36]

LUNAN, JAMES, weaver in Purgavie, Lintrathen, soldier of Ogilvy's
Regiment 1745.[OR36]

LUNAN, JOHN, weaver in Loanhead of Lour, Forfar, soldier of Ogilvy's
Regiment 1745. [OR36]

LUNDIE, JOHN, workman in Kirriemuir, soldier of Ogilvy's Regiment
1745.[OR36]

LYON, CHARLES, son of James Lyon innkeeper, soldier 1745. [LPR222]

LYON, CHARLES, apprentice silversmith in Dundee, soldier 1745.
[LPR222]

LYON, DAVID, vintner in Montrose, prisoner in Montrose, Canongate
and Carlisle 1746. [LPR174][P2.354]

LYON, JAMES, innkeeper in Dundee, soldier of Ogilvy's Regiment 1745.
[OR36][LPR222]

LYON, JAMES, tailor in Montrose, prisoner in Arbroath 1746. [P2.354]

LYON, JOHN, Earl of Strathmore, born 1690, fought and died at
Sheriffmuir 13.11.1715. [SP.VIII.306]

LYON, J......, taken prisoner after Sheriffmuir 13.11.1715. [CAT.205]

LYON, PATRICK, of Auchterhouse, son of the Earl of Strathmore,
Lieutenant Colonel of Panmure's Foot, 1715, killed at Sheriffmuir
13.11.1715.[SRO.GD45.1.201][JAB10][[CAT.205][SP.VIII.303]

LYON, PATRICK, a proprietor's son in Ogil, Tannadice, Lieutenant of
Ogilvy's Regiment 1745. [OR4][LPR220]

LYON, PHILIP, transported from Liverpool to South Carolina on the
Wakefield 21.4.1716. [SPC.1716.309][CTB.31.205]

LYON, ROBERT, Ensign of Panmure's Foot, 1715. [SRO.GD45.1.201]

LYON, WILLIAM, Lieutenant in Strathmore's Battalion, a prisoner in
Preston, transported from Liverpool to Jamaica or Virginia on the
Elizabeth and Ann 29.6.1716, landed in Virginia 1716.
[SPC.1716.310][CS.V.162][VSP.1.186]

LYON, ..., son of George Lyon minister in Tannadice, "hung as a rebel
171.." [F.3.305]

THE JACOBITES OF

ANGUS

1689-1746

[Part Two]

by David Dobson

THE JACOBITES OF ANGUS
Part Two [M to Y]

MACARRA, JAMES, servant in Balnakeely, Lintrathen, soldier of
Ogilvy's Regiment 1745. [OR37]

MCCOY, JAMES, weaver, soldier of Ogilvy's Regiment 1745, prisoner in
Carlisle 1745. [P3.30]

MACDONALD, JOHN, servant in Dundee, soldier of Ogilvy's Regiment
1745.[OR37]

MACDOUGALL, SAMUEL, workman in Kingoldrum, soldier of Ogilvy's
Regiment 1745. [OR37]

MACDUFF, JAMES, of Turfachie, Tannadice, the younger, Lieutenant of
Ogilvy's Regiment 1745. a prisoner. [OR4]

MACKAY, ROBERT, soldier of Ogilvy's Regiment 1745, a prisoner.
[OR37]

MACKENZIE, PATRICK, servant in Torbeg, Forfar, soldier of Ogilvy's
Regiment 1745. [OR47]

MCKENZIE, ROBERT, born 1722, soldier of Ogilvy's Regiment 1745,
prisoner in Inverness 1746. [P3.132]

MACKIE, ALEXANDER, in Arbroath, soldier of Ogilvy's Regiment
1745. [OR37]

MACKIE, ROBERT, ostler, servant to Alexander Low in Brechin, 1745,
prisoner in Montrose, Inverness and Tilbury. [LPR180][P3.110]

MACKIE, WILLIAM, in Montrose, soldier of Ogilvy's Regiment 1745,
prisoner in Montrose 1746. [OR37][LPR320]

MACINTOSH, WILLIAM, servant in Dundee, soldier of Ogilvy's
Regiment 1745. [OR37]

MACNICOLL, WILLIAM, workman in Cramieburn, Kirriemuir, soldier
of Ogilvy's Regiment 1745. [OR37]

MACNICOLL, WILLIAM, workman in Runtalive, Kirriemuir, soldier of
Ogilvy's Regiment 1745. [OR37]

MAIN, WILLIAM, farmer in Newton of Panbride, soldier of Ogilvy's Regiment 1745, a prisoner in Arbroath 1746. [OR38] [P3.4]

MAITLAND, JAMES, in Careston, escaped to Sweden 1746. [GK115]

MAITLAND, JOHN, Episcopal preacher in Pitforkie, Careston, Chaplain of Ogilvy's Regiment 1745. [OR7][LPR180]

MALCOLM, WILLIAM, workman in Kingoldrum, soldier of Ogilvy's Regiment 1745.[OR38]

MANN, ALEXANDER, jr., servant in Moss-side of Lour, Forfar, soldier of Ogilvy's Regiment 1745. [OR38]

MARSHALL, JAMES, official to the Earl of Airlie in Auchterhouse, soldier of Ogilvy's Regiment 1745, prisoner in Dundee 1746. [OR38][P3.4]

MARTIN, DAVID, born 1708, weaver in Montrose, soldier of Ogilvy's Regiment 1745, prisoner in Montrose and Tilbury, died 1746. [OR38][LPR320]

MARTIN, JOHN, Lady Ogilvy's servant, prisoner in Edinburgh Castle 1746.[P3.10]

MASTERTON, ALEXANDER, weaver in Forfar, soldier of Ogilvy's Regiment 1745.[OR38]

MATHER, ALEXANDER, brewer in Brechin, Ensign of Ogilvy's Regiment 1745, a prisoner. [OR6]

MATHER, ALEXANDER, born 1732, son of David Mather baker in Brechin, soldier of Ogilvy's Regiment 1745, escaped 1746. [OR38][P3.10]

MATHER, CHARLES, wright in Kirriemuir, soldier of Ogilvy's Regiment 1745. [OR38]

MATHER, CHARLES, born 1725, ploughman in Braideston, Airlie, soldier of Ogilvy's Regiment 1745, prisoner in Montrose and Tilbury 1746. [OR38][P3.12]

MATHER, DAVID, son of David Mather baker in Brechin. soldier of Ogilvy's Regiment 1745. [OR38]

MATHER, GEORGE, son of David Mather baker in Brechin, soldier of Ogilvy's Regiment 1745. [OR38]

MATHER, JAMES, merchant in Brechin, Ensign in Ogilvy's Regiment, a prisoner in Brechin and Montrose1746. [LPR180][P3.12]

MATHIE, JAMES, born 1724, ploughman in Old Montrose, soldier of Ogilvy's Regiment 1745, died in prison.[OR39][P3.12]

MATTHEW, ANDREW, born 14.1.1693, Auchterhouse, transported 8.5.1747.[P.3.12]

MAULE, GEORGE, son of Patrick Maule and Christian Forbes, factor for the Earl of Panmure, a prisoner in Carlisle 1716. [JAB.155][StAUL.Cheap MS.5/537]

MAULE, HARRY, of Kellie, son of George Maule the Earl of Panmure, fought at Sheriffmuir 13.11.1715, escaped to Holland, died 23.6.1734. [SP.VII.22][CRA.233]

MAULE, JAMES, Earl of Panmure, son of George Maule, Colonel of Panmure's Foot, 1715, fought at Sheriffmuir 13.11.1715, escaped via Montrose to France, died in Paris 6.4.1720. [SRO.GD45.1.201][SP.VII.26][CRA.233]

MAULE, PATRICK, minister in Panbride, deposed 1716. [HHA.171][F.3.448][SRO.CH2.15.3]

MEAL, JOHN, ploughman in Newton of Glamis, soldier of Ogilvy's Regiment 1745.[OR39]

MILL, DAVID, servant to Alexander Madison in Bulzeon, Liff, soldier of Ogilvy's Regiment 1745. [OR39]

MILL, DAVID, weaver in Newbigging, Newtyle, soldier of Ogilvy's Regiment 1745.[OR39]

MILL, JAMES, ploughman in Glamis, soldier of Ogilvy's Regiment 1745. [OR39]

MILL, JAMES, ploughman in Newton of Airlie, soldier of Ogilvy's Regiment 1745, possibly transported from Liverpool to Virginia on the Johnson 22.4.1747, landed at Port Oxford, Maryland, 5.8.1747. [OR39][PRO.T1.328]

MILL, JOHN, in Montrose, soldier of Ogilvy's Regiment 1745, a prisoner. [OR39]

MILL, ROBERT, ploughman in Reedie, Airlie, soldier of Ogilvy's Regiment 1745.[OR39]

MILLER, DAVID, jr., shoemaker in Brechin, soldier of Ogilvy's Regiment 1745. [OR39]

MILLER, DUNCAN, weaver in Auchmithie, soldier in Ogilvy's Regiment 1745. [OR39]

MILLER, JAMES, horsehirer in Dundee, soldier of Ogilvy's Regiment 1745.[OR39]

MILLER, JOHN, ploughman in Glamis, soldier of Ogilvy's Regiment 1745, prisoner in Montrose 1746. [OR40][P3.192]

MILLER, PATRICK, from Burnside, soldier of Ogilvy's Regiment 1745, prisoner in Burnside and Montrose 1746. [P3.194]

MILLER, WILLIAM, Captain in Strathmore's Battalion, a prisoner in Preston 1716.[CS.V.162]

MILLER, WILLIAM, sailor in Dundee, soldier of Ogilvy's Regiment 1745, prisoner in Leith, Edinburgh, Carlisle, and York 1746. [OR40][P3.196]

MILNE, ALEXANDER, shepherd in Bonnyton, Maryton, soldier in Ogilvy's Regiment 1745. [OR40]

MILNE, GEORGE, farmer in Balcathie, Arbirlot, Lieutenant of Ogilvy's Regiment 1745. [OR5]

MILNE, JAMES, jr., farmer's son in Landsend, Logie, Kirriemuir, soldier of Ogilvy's Regiment 1745. [OR40]

MILNE, JOHN, doctor and surgeon in Montrose, prisoner in Montrose, Stirling and Edinburgh 1746-1747. [P3.196]

MILNE, JOHN, town officer of Montrose, prisoner in Montrose and Stirling 1746.[P3.198]

MILNE, ROBERT, servant to William Smith in Kirriemuir, soldier of Ogilvy's Regiment 1745. [OR40]

MILNE, THOMAS, workman in Burn of Lednathie, Kirriemuir, soldier of Ogilvy's Regiment 1745. [OR40]

MILNE, WILLIAM, of Bonnyton, Montrose, 1745. [LPR178]

MITCHELL, ALEXANDER, ploughman in Balgownie, Eassie, soldier of Ogilvy's Regiment 1745. [OR40]

MITCHELL, DAVID, born 1686, soldier of Ogilvy's Regiment 1745, prisoner in Inverness 1746. [P3.198]

MITCHELL, JAMES, born 1706 in Panmure, blacksmith in Benshie, soldier of Ogilvy's Regiment 1745, prisoner in Montrose, Inverness, and Tilbury.[P3.200]

MITCHELL, JOHN, born 1730, workman in Dundee, drummer boy of Ogilvy's Regiment 1745, a prisoner in Dundee. [OR8][LPR224]

MITCHELL, JOHN, wright in Forfar, soldier of Ogilvy's Regiment 1745, killed. [OR40]

MITCHELL, THOMAS, buttonmaker in Dundee, Sergeant of Ogilvy's Regiment 1745. [OR9]

MITCHELL, WILLIAM, skipper in Dundee, prisoner in Dundee 1746. [P3.202]

MONCUR, ANDREW, weaver in Easter Kinnordy, Kirriemuir, soldier of Ogilvy's Regiment 1745. [OR40]

MONCUR, PATRICK, ploughman in Nevay, Eassie, soldier of Ogilvy's Regiment 1745. [OR40]

MONEY, GEORGE, ploughman in Arniefoul, Glamis, soldier of Ogilvy's Regiment 1745. [OR40]

MOONIE, THOMAS, ploughman in Cossins, Glamis, soldier of Ogilvy's Regiment 1745. [OR41]

MOORE, WILLIAM, horsehirer in Dundee, soldier of Ogilvy's Regiment 1745. [OR40]

MORGAN, DAVID, a servant in Dundee, drummer of Ogilvy's Regiment 1745, a prisoner in Dundee. [OR8][P3.208]

MORTIMER, JAMES, born 1728, servant to Rattray of Drummie, soldier of Ogilvy's Regiment 1745, prisoner in Inverness and Kent. [OR41][P3.212]

MOUAT, WILLIAM, born in Montrose 1706, soldier of Ogilvy's Regiment 1745, prisoner in Montrose and Carlisle, transported. [LPR178/320][P3.30][P3.214]

MUDIE, DAVID, from Glamis, soldier of Ogilvy's regiment 1745, prisoner in Montrose 1746-1747. [P3.214]

MUDIE, JAMES, from Arbroath, Ensign of Ogilvy's Regiment 1745, prisoner in Montrose 1746-1747. [P3.214]

MUDIE, JAMES, born 1717 son of John Mudie and Margaret Ogilvie, in Auchmithie, soldier of Ogilvy's Regiment 1745, a prisoner in Inverness and London. [OR41][P3.206]

MUDIE, THOMAS, ploughman in Baikie, Airlie, soldier of Ogilvy's Regiment 1745.[OR41]

MUDIE, THOMAS, weaver in Dundee, soldier in Ogilvy's Regiment 1745. [OR41]

MYLES, JAMES, workman in Kingoldrum, soldier of Ogilvy's Regiment 1745.[OR41]

MYLES, JAMES, servant in Glamis, soldier of Ogilvy's Regiment 1745. [OR41]

NAIRN, GEORGE, surgeon of Panmure's Foot, 1715. [SRO.GD45.1.201]

NAIRN, GEORGE, brother to the laird of Baldovan, Ensign of Panmure's Foot, 1715. [SRO.GD45.1.201]

NAIRN, ROBERT, soldier of Ogilvy's Regiment, 1745, a prisoner. [OR42]

NAIRN, WILLIAM, of Baldovan, Captain of Panmure's Foot, 1715. [SRO.GD45.1.201]

NAISMITH, JOHN, born 22.3.1726 in Dundee, son of Robert Naismith and Jean Young, a woolweaver in Dundee, soldier in Ogilvy's Regiment 1745, prisoner in Stirling and Carlisle 1746, transported from Liverpool to Virginia on the Johnson 22.4.1747, landed at Port Oxford, Maryland, 5.8.1747. [P.3.224][PRO.T1.328]

NAISMITH, ROBERT, from Dundee, soldier of Ogilvy's Regiment 1745, prisoner in Stirling and Carlisle 1746. [P3.224]

NAPIER, JAMES, carter in Montrose, prisoner in Montrose and Stirling 1746. [P3.224]

NAPIER, JAMES, from Arbroath, soldier of Ogilvy's Regiment 1745, prisoner in Arbroath 1746-1747. [P3.224]

NASH, JOHN, servant in Dundee, soldier of Ogilvy's Regiment 1745. [OR42]

NASH, WILLIAM, servant in Dundee, soldier of Ogilvy's Regiment 1745.
    [OR42]

NEVAY, DAVID, servant in Forfar, soldier of Ogilvy's Regiment 1745.
    [OR42]

NICOL, JAMES, tailor in Arbroath, soldier of Ogilvy's Regiment 1745.
    [OR42]

NICHOLL, JAMES, born 20.1.1723 in Brechin, son of William Nicholl
    and Margaret Margaret Gourlay, ploughman in Brechin, soldier in
    Ogilvy's Regiment 1745, prisoner in Inverness and Tilbury,
    transported from London to Barbados on the Frere 20.3.1747.
    [P.3.226]

NICOL, JOHN, born 1722, soldier of Ogilvy's Regiment 1745, prisoner at
    Culloden.   [OR42][P3.226]

OGILVY, ALEXANDER, jr., in Braes of Lintrathen, soldier of Ogilvy's
    Regiment 1745, prisoner in Carlisle, Chester and York, pardoned on
    enlistment 1748.   [OR42][P3.226]

OGILVIE, DAVID, son of David Ogilvie Earl of Airlie and Grizel Lyon,
    died 12.1.1731. [SP.1.127]

OGILVIE, DAVID, Earl of Airlie, Colonel of Ogilvy's Regiment,
    escaped via Bergen and Sweden to France 1746. [OR1][GK111

OGILVY, DAVID, merchant in Coul, Tannadice, Captain of Ogilvy's
    Regiment 1745, escaped from Dundee to Norway 1746, prisoner in
    Bergen, later in France. [OR2/127][LPR228]

OGILVY, DAVID, of Pool, Lintrathen, Life Guards 1745, prisoner in
    Aberdeen and Edinburgh, escaped 12.1746. [LPR228][P3.236]

OGILVY, DAVID, farmer' s son in Shannaly, Lintrathen, Lieutenant of
    Ogilvy's Regiment 1745, prisoner in Edinburgh 1746-1747.
    [OR5][P3.236]

OGILVY, DAVID, labourer in Kirriemuir, soldier of Ogilvy's Regiment
    1745, a prisoner in Carlisle, died in York prison 9.6.1747.
    [OR42][LPR226][P3.236]

OGILVY, FRANCIS, merchant in Montrose, prisoner in Montrose and
    Stirling 1746.[P3.238]

OGILVIE, HENRY, Ensign of Strathmore's Battalion, a prisoner at
    Preston 1716,transported from Liverpool to St Kitts on the
    Hockenhill 25.6.1716, mutineed and landed on St Martins, Dutch
    Virgin Islands, 9.1716.
    [CS.V.162][JAB.21][SPC.1716.312][CTB.31.2..]

OGILVY, HENRY, innkeeper in Dundee, 1745, prisoner in Dundee.
    [LPR228]

OGILVY, JAMES, miller in the Mill of Inshewan, Tannadice, Lieutenant of Ogilvy's Regiment 1745, escaped to Norway, prisoner in Bergen, later in Sweden. [OR5][LPR228][GK117]

OGILVY, JAMES, from Monikie, soldier of Ogilvy's Regiment 1745, prisoner in Montrose 1746-1747. [P3.238]

OGILVY, JAMES, appointed a Colonel in service of James VIII 9.10.1723. [JP245]

OGILVY, JAMES, labourer in Meams, Kirriemuir, soldier of Ogilvy's Regiment 1745.   [OR42]

OGILVY, JAMES, servant in Forfar, soldier of Ogilvy's Regiment 1745. [OR43]

OGILVY, JAMES, tinsmith in Barry, soldier of Ogilvy's Regiment 1745, prisoner after Culloden. [OR43][P3.238]

OGILVY, JOHN, born 1721, soldier of Ogilvy's Regiment 1745, prisoner in Perth, Canongate and Carlisle, transported from Liverpool to Virginia on the Gildart 24.2.1747, landed at Port North Potomac, Maryland, 5.8.1747. [OR43][P.3.238][PRO.T1.328]

OGILVIE, JOHN, born 1699, son of David Ogilvie Earl of Airlie and Grizel Lyon, died 24.7.1761. [SP.1.127]

OGILVY, JOHN, of Inshewan, Tannadice, Paymaster and Captain of Ogilvy's Regiment, escaped to Norway, prisoner in Bergen, later in France 1746. [OR2][LPR228]

OGILVY, JOHN, of Inshewan, Tannadice, born 1711 son of John Ogilvy and Mary Keith, Captain of Ogilvy's Regiment 1745, escaped from Dundee via Norway to France 1746, died 1781. [OR2/140]

OGILVY, JOHN, farmer in Wester Lethnot, Cortachy, Captain of Ogilvy's Regiment 1745. [OR2]

OGILVY, JOHN, farmer in Lochmill, Glamis, Captain of Ogilvy's Regiment 1745.   [OR3]

OGILVY, JOHN, of Rochilhill, Glamis, Lieutenant of Ogilvy's Regiment 1745, died ca.1774. [OR5]

OGILVY, JOHN, of Quick, Cortachy, Ensign of Ogilvy's Regiment 1745, a prisoner.[OR6][P3.238]

OGILVY, JOHN, labourer in Cortachy, soldier of Ogilvy's Regiment 1745, prisoner in Carlisle, Chester and London, discharged.[P3.238]

OGILVY, Lady MARGARET, of Airlie, wife of Lord Ogilvy, prisoner in Inverness and Edinburgh, escaped 21.11.1746, died in France 1757 [P3.240]

OGILVY, THOMAS, of Inverquharity, Kirriemuir, third son of Sir John Ogilvy and Helen Mercer, Captain of Ogilvy's Regiment 1745, escaped from Dundee via Bergen to France 1746. [OR3/127/142][LPR226]

OGILVIE, THOMAS, merchant in Dundee, Captain 1745, prisoner in
Alloa and Edinburgh 1746. [P3.240]

OGILVY, THOMAS, of East Mill, Glen Isla, Captain of Ogilvy's
Regiment 1745, prisoner in Edinburgh Castle 1746-1751, died
escaping during 1751. [OR3/143][LPR226][P3.240]

OGILVY, THOMAS, the younger, of East Mill, Glen Isla, born 1725,
Ensign of Ogilvy's Regiment 1745, escaped to France, returned to
Scotland 1747, died 5.6.1765. [OR6/145]

OGILVY, THOMAS, farmer in Little Kenny, Kingoldrum, Lieutenant of
Ogilvy's Regiment 1745. [OR5][LPR228]

OGILVY, WILLIAM, farmer in Meikle Kenny, Kingoldrum, Captain of
Ogilvy's Regiment 1745. [OR3]

OGILVY, WILLIAM, servant at the Mill of Meathie, Inverarity, soldier of
Ogilvy's Regiment 1745. [OR43]

OGILVY, WILLIAM, born 1730, dyer in Forfar, transport driver of
Ogilvy's Regiment 1745, prisoner in Dundee, Carlisle and York
1746-1747. [OR43][P3.242]

OLIPHANT, JOHN, baillie of Dundee, Grenadier Captain of Panmure's
Foot, 1715, in Amsterdam 6.1716, by 1719 in Brussels.
[SRO.GD45.1.201.1.1]

ORKNEY, JOHN, shipmaster in Montrose, prisoner there 1746.
[LPR320][P3.242]

ORKNEY, JOHN, shipmaster in Montrose, prisoner there 1746. [LPR320]

ORMSBIE, JOHN, in Lunan, soldier of Ogilvy's Regiment 1745, prisoner
in Arbroath 1746. [P3.244]

ORROCK, ALEXANDER, Lieutenant in Strathmore's Battalion, a
prisoner in Preston 1716, transported from Liverpool to Virginia on
the Goodspeed 28.7.1716, landed in Maryland 10.1716.
[SPC.1716.310][CTB.31.209][HM.388]

ORROCK, JOHN, Customs officer in Dundee 1745. [LPR228]

OUCHTERLONY, ALEXANDER, son of the laird of Guynd, Ensign of
Panmure's Foot, 1715. [SRO.GD45.1.201]

OUCHTERLONY, ALEXANDER, writer in Arbroath, prisoner there
1746-1747. [P2.16]

OUCHTERLONY, JAMES, baillie of Montrose, Ensign of Panmure's
Foot, 1715.[SRO.GD45.1.201]

OUCHTERLONY, JOHN, mason in Dundee, soldier of Ogilvy's Regiment
1745. [LPR228][OR42]

OUCHTERLONY, JOHN, apprentice writer in Montrose, prisoner there
1746.[LPR320]

OUCHTERLONY, PATRICK, Lieutenant of Panmure's Foot, 1715.
[SRO.GD45.1.201]

OUCHTERLONY, PETER, coffee-house keeper in Dundee, Life Guard 1745, prisoner in Dundee 1746. [LPR228/351]

OUCHTERLONY, ROBERT, of the Guynd, Episcopal preacher in St Vigean's 1715.[HHA.170][SRO.CH2.575.1]

OUCHTERLONY, ROBERT, merchant in Montrose, prisoner in Montrose and Stirling 1746-1747. [P2.16]

OUCHTERLONY, ..., taken prisoner at Sheriffmuir 13.11.1715. [CAT.205]

PALMER, JOHN, born 1723, workman in Arbroath, soldier in Ogilvy's Regiment 1745, soldier in Holland,died in Arbroath 13.5.1811. [HHA174][OR42/146]

PALMER, ROBERT, workman in Hillside, Kirriemuir, soldier of Ogilvy's Regiment 1745. [OR43]

PALMER, ROBERT, workman in Dalairn, Clova, soldier of Ogilvy's Regiment 1745.[OR43]

PALMER, WILLIAM, farmer's son in Buckhood, Kirriemuir, soldier of Ogilvy's Regiment 1745. [OR43]

PANTON, JAMES, Ensign of Panmure's Foot, 1715. [SRO.GD45.1.201]

PATERSON, ALEXANDER, servant to the Earl of Airlie, in Auchterhouse, soldier of Ogilvy's Regiment 1745. [OR43]

PATERSON, ALEXANDER, servant to the laird of Burnside in Grange of Monifieth, soldier 1745, a prisoner in Dundee. [LPR230]

PATERSON, JAMES, workman in Dundee, soldier of Ogilvy's Regiment 1745, a prisoner in Dundee. [OR43]

PATTULLO, GEORGE, merchant in Dundee, Ensign of Ogilvy's Regiment 1745. [OR6]

PATTULLO, HENRY, merchant in Dundee, muster master 1745, escaped from Dundee via Bergen and Sweden to France 1746. [LPR230][GK118][OR127]

PEDDIE, JOHN, born 1708 son of John Peddie, workman in Kinclune, Kingoldrum, soldier of Ogilvy's Regiment 1745. [OR44]

PEDDIE. JOHN, born 6.7.1703 in Arbroath, son of John Peddie and Jean Smith, transported from Liverpool to Virginia on the Gildart 24.2.1747, landed at Port North Potomac, Maryland, 5.8.1747. [P.2.250][PRO.T1.328]

PIERSON, ALEXANDER, shipmaster in Arbroath, prisoner in Arbroath and Montrose 1746. [P3.250]

PETRIE, ANDREW, workman in Dundee, soldier of Ogilvy's Regiment 1745.[OR44]

PETRIE, JAMES, born 1727, labourer, soldier of Ogilvy's Regiment 1745, prisoner in Carlisle and Lancaster, transported from Liverpool to the Leeward Islands on the Veteran 5.5.1747, liberated and landed on Martinique 6.1747.[P.3.250][PRO.SP36.102]

PHILP, JAMES, of Almerieclose, Arbroath, son of James Philp and Margaret Graham, Standard Bearer to James Graham of Claverhouse at Killiecrankie 1689.   [HHA163]

PHILP, JOHN, of Almerieclose, Arbroath, son of James Philp, escaped to Holland in 1716, joined the New Dutch West India Company, appointed Governor of St Martins, Dutch West Indies, 1728. [Goslinga, 136]

PHILP, JOHN, carrier in Forfar, soldier of Ogilvy's Regiment 1745. [LPR230]

PIGGOT, ALEXANDER, servant to Mrs Lyon of Bridgend, Kingoldrum, soldier of Ogilvy's Regiment, a prisoner. [OR44]

PIGGOT, ALEXANDER, born 1721, a workman in Bridge End, Kingoldrum, soldier 1745, prisoner in Inverness, transported from London to Jamaica on the Carteret or the St George 31.3.1747, landed in Jamaica 1747. [LPR230][P.3.252][PRO.CO137.58]

PINKERTON, JAMES, born 1714 in Montrose, saddler in Edinburgh, prisoner in Montrose, Inverness and Tilbury 1746. [P3.252]

PITSCOTTIE, JAMES, Lieutenant of Panmure's Foot, 1715. [SRO.GD45.1.201]

PROCTOR, PETER, workman in Glen Ogilvy, soldier of Ogilvy's Regiment 1745.   [OR44]

PROPHET, THOMAS, workman in Balmuckity, Kirriemuir, soldier of Ogilvy's Regiment 1745. [OR44]

PYOT, ALEXANDER, wright in Montrose, soldier of Ogilvy's Regiment 1745. [OR44]

PYOT, DAVID, wright in Montrose, prisoner there 1746. [LPR320]

RAE CHARLES, workman in Kingoldrum, soldier of Ogilvy's Regiment 1745.[OR44]

RAE, JAMES, servant in Glamis, soldier of Ogilvy's Regiment 1745. [OR44]

RAIT, FRANCIS, son of John Rait minister in Inverkeiller, minister in Kinnaird, Angus, ca.1716. [F.3.395]

RAIT, JOHN, minister in Inverkeilor and in Lunan, died 1730. [F.3.439][HHA.170]

RAIT, WILLIAM, of Pitforthar, born 1648 son of William Rait minister in Monikie, died 1741. [F.5.365]

RAIT, WILLIAM, surgeon in Dundee, son of Dr Rait, surgeon of the Life Guards, 1745. [LPR232]

RAMSAY, ALEXANDER, Ensign in Strathmore's Battalion, a prisoner in Preston 1716. [CS.V.162]

RAMSAY, ALEXANDER, shoemaker in Brechin, soldier of Ogilvy's Regiment 1745. [OR45]

RAMSAY, ANDREW, a former Ensign in Strathmore's Battalion, appointed as a Captain of Foot 22.4.1726. [JP245]

RAMSAY, DAVID, of Cairntoun, Lieutenant of Panmure's Foot, 1715. [SRO.GD45.1.201][HHA.167]

RAMSAY, DAVID, workman in Fornathy, Linlathen, soldier of Ogilvy's Regiment 1745. [OR45]

RAMSAY, GEORGE, weaver in Dundee, soldier of Ogilvy's Regiment 1745.[OR45]

RAMSAY, JAMES, jr., tailor in Forfar, soldier of Ogilvy's Regiment 1745. [OR45]

RAMSAY, JOHN, crofter in Carseburn, Forfar, soldier of Ogilvy's Regiment 1745. [OR45]

RAMSAY, JOHN, merchant in Dundee, prisoner in Dundee 1746. [P3.260]

RAMSAY, PATRICK, in Cortachy, prisoner in Stirling 1746-1747.[P3.260]

RAMSAY, ROBERT, weaver in Balmaw, Newtyle, soldier of Ogilvy's Regiment 1745. [OR45]

RAMSAY, ..., in Pearsie, Kingoldrum, soldier of Ogilvy's Regiment 1745. [OR45]

RATTRAY, CHARLES, of Denoon, Glamis, soldier of Ogilvy's Regiment 1745, prisoner in Dundee 1746. [LPR351][OR45]

RATTRAY, CHARLES, jr., in Denoon, Glamis, Ensign of Ogilvy's Regiment 1745. [OR7]

RATTRAY, JAMES, ropemaker in Dundee, clerk to the Depute Governor of Dundee, 1745. [LPR232]

REID, ALEXANDER, servant in Brechin, soldier of Ogilvy's Regiment 1745. [OR45]

REID, DAVID, workman in Myre End, Kingoldrum, soldier of Ogilvy's Regiment 1745, prisoner in Carlisle, transported 1747. [OR45][P.3.266][LPR230]

REID, GEORGE, cottar in Drums, Brechin, soldier of Ogilvy's Regiment 1745.[OR45]

REID, JAMES, born 1729, labourer in Angus, soldier of Ogilvy's Regiment 1745, transported from Liverpool to the Leeward Islands on the Veteran 5.5.1747, liberated and landed on Martinique 6.1747. [PRO.T1.328][[P.3.266][OR45]

REID, PETER, brewer in Montrose, soldier of Ogilvy's Regiment 1745. [OR46]

REID, ROBERT, jr., shoemaker in Brechin, soldier of Ogilvy's Regiment 1745. [OR45]

REID, ROBERT, in Kinnaber, soldier of Ogilvy's Regiment 1745, prisoner in Montrose and Edinburgh 1746. [P3.268]

REID, WILLIAM, born 1720, groom to Hunter of Burnside, Monifieth, Life Guard 1745, prisoner in Inverness and Tilbury 1746. [LPR234][P3.268]

REID, WILLIAM, weaver in Kinnaber, prisoner in Montrose 1746-1747. [P3.268]

RENNY, ALEXANDER, merchant in Montrose, prisoner in Montrose and Stirling 1746-1747. [P3.270]

RENNY, JAMES, merchant in Montrose, prisoner in Montrose and Stirling 1746-1747. [P3.270]

RENWICK, ANDREW, ploughman in Kinnettles, soldier of Ogilvy's Regiment 1745. [OR46]

REOCH, JAMES, innkeeper in Glen Isla, Sergeant of Ogilvy's Regiment 1745. [OR9]

RETTIE, JAMES, servant in Farnell, soldier of Ogilvy's Regiment 1745. [OR46]

RITCHIE, ALEXANDER, threadmaker in Arbroath, soldier of Ogilvy's Regiment 1745, prisoner in Arbroath, Dundee, Canongate and Carlisle 1746-1747, transported 1747. [OR46][P3.274]

RITCHIE, JAMES, horse hirer in Forfar, soldier of Ogilvy's Regiment 1745. [OR46]

RITCHIE, PETER, servant in Leuchland, Brechin, soldier of Ogilvy's Regiment 1745. [OR46]

RITCHIE, WILLIAM, chapman in Burn of Arrat, Brechin, soldier of Ogilvy's Regiment 1745. [OR46]

ROBB, JAMES, servant in Baikie, Airlie, soldier of Ogilvy's regiment 1745. [OR46]

ROBERTSON, ALEXANDER, a sergeant of Ogilvy's Regiment 1745, prisoner in Montrose 1746. [P3.274]

ROBERTSON, ALEXANDER, ploughman in Letham Cotton, St Vigeans, soldier of Ogilvy's Regiment 1745, prisoner at Culloden and Montrose. [OR46][P3.274]

ROBERTSON, ALEXANDER, merchant in Dundee, 1745. [LPR232]

ROBERTSON, ANDREW, soldier of Ogilvy's Regiment 1745, servant to
Major Glasgow, prisoner at Culloden and London. [OR47][P3.276]

ROBERTSON, CHARLES, servant in Nevay, Eassie, soldier of Ogilvy's
Regiment 1745. [OR47]

ROBERTSON, DONALD, workman in Glen Prosen, soldier of Ogilvy's
Regiment 1745. [OR47]

ROBERTSON, GILBERT, Ensign of Panmure's Foot, 1715.
[SRO.GD45.1.201]

ROBERTSON, JAMES, servant in Rossie, Montrose, soldier of Ogilvy's
Regiment 1745. [OR47]

ROBERTSON, JOHN, farmer in Crandart, Glen Isla, Captain of Ogilvy's
Regiment 1745. [OR3/153]

ROBERTSON, JOHN, servant in Thornton, Glamis, soldier of Ogilvy's
Regiment 1745. [OR47]

ROBERTSON, PETER, apprentice in Dundee, soldier of Ogilvy's
Regiment 1745. [OR47]

ROBERTSON, ..., schoolmaster in Kinnell, deposed 3.1716.
[SRO.CH2.15.3]

ROBIN, WILLIAM, servant to Lord Airlie's second son in Dundee,
soldier of Ogilvy's Regiment 1745. [OR46]

ROBINSON, ALEXANDER, born 1711, soldier of Ogilvy's Regiment
1745, prisoner in Inverness and Tilbury, transported 1747. [P3.280]

ROGER, JAMES, farmer, prisoner in Stirling and Edinburgh 1746-1747.
[P3.282]

ROGER, JOHN, servant in Lightnie, Lethnot, soldier of Ogilvy's Regiment
1745, prisoner in Montrose 1746.[OR47][P3.284]

ROGER, PETER, servant in Lightnie, Lethnot, soldier of Ogilvy's
Regiment 1745. [OR47]

ROSS, PATRICK, Episcopal minister in Arbroath 1715. [JAB.243]

ROSS, THOMAS, former sergeant of Lascelles Regiment - a deserter,
prisoner in Edinburgh 1746-1747. [P3.290]

ROUGH, ALEXANDER, servant in Glen Ogilvy, soldier of Ogilvy's
Regiment 1745. [OR47]

ROUGH, THOMAS, in Eassie, soldier of Ogilvy's Regiment 1745.
[OR47]

ROY, JOHN, servant in Lednathie, Kirriemuir, soldier of Ogilvy's
Regiment 1745. [OR47]

RUSSELL, JOHN, born 1723, sail-weaver in Backmuir, Barry, soldier of
Ogilvy's Regiment 1745, prisoner at Culloden, Arbroath, Dundee,
Canongate, Carlisle, transported from Liverpool to Virginia on the
Gildart 24.2.1747, landed at Port North Potomac, Maryland,
5.8.1747. [OR47][P3.294][PRO.T1.328]

SALTER, WILLIAM, victualler and maltman in Dundee, prisoner in Dundee 1746. [LPR236][P3.298]

SAMSON, ANDREW, in Glen Isla, prisoner in Dundee 1746. [P3.298]

SAMSON, PATRICK, in Burnside, soldier of Ogilvy's Regiment 1745, prisoner in Montrose 1746. [P3.298]

SAMSON, WILLIAM, workman in Lintrathen, Sergeant of Ogilvy's Regiment 1745.[OR10]

SANDERS, JAMES, in Aberlemno, soldier of Ogilvy's Regiment 1745, prisoner in Montrose 1746. [P3.298]

SANDIMAN, ANDREW, workman in Caldhame, Brechin, soldier of Ogilvy's Regiment 1745. [OR48]

SCOTT, ANDREW, servant to Mr Comrie, prisoner in Stirling 1746. [P3.300]

SCOTT, CHARLES, ploughman in Glamis, 1745. [LPR234]

SCOTT, DAVID, crofter in West Dod, Forfar, soldier of Ogilvy's Regiment 1745.   [OR48]

SCOTT, DAVID, tailor in Arbroath, soldier of Ogilvy's Regiment 1745, a prisoner in Stirling 1746, transported from Liverpool to Virginia on the Gildart 24.2.1747, landed at Port North Potomac, Maryland, 5.8.1747. [OR48][P.3.300][PRO.T1.328]

SCOTT, DAVID, ploughman in Balcathie, Arbirlot, soldier of Ogilvy's Regiment 1745, prisoner in Arbroath 1746. [OR48][P3.300]

SCOTT, DAVID, pendicler in West Dod, Forfar, soldier of Ogilvy's Regiment 1745, prisoner in Montrose 1746. [P3.302]

SCOTT, JAMES, soldier of Ogilvy's Regiment 1745, a prisoner. [OR48]

SCOTT, JOHN, merchant in Montrose, soldier of Ogilvy's Regiment, Governor of Montrose 1745, prisoner there 1746, escaped to Sweden 1746. [OR48][GK118][LPR320]

SCOTT, JOHN, cooper in Brechin, soldier of Ogilvy's Regiment 1745. [OR48]

SCOTT, PATRICK, in Burnside, soldier of Ogilvy's Regiment 1745, prisoner in   Montrose 1746. [P3.302]

SCOTT, ROBERT, salmon fisher, prisoner in Montrose, Stirling and Edinburgh 1746. [P3.304]

SCRIMGEOUR, GEORGE, Captain in Strathmore's Battalion, a prisoner in Preston 1716. [CS.V.162]

SEATON, ANDREW, chapman in Alyth, soldier of Ogilvy's Regiment 1745. [OR48]

SETON, WILLIAM, non-jurant Episcopal minister in Forfar 1745, prisoner in Montrose 1746. [LPR234][P3.306]

SHANKS, DAVID, weaver in Arbroath, soldier of Ogilvy's Regiment 1745. [OR48]

SHANKS, JOHN, weaver in Arbroath, soldier of Ogilvy's Regiment 1745, a prisoner in Stirling. [OR48][LPR188]

SHAW, ALEXANDER, farmer in Achavan, Glen Isla, son of Duncan Shaw of Crathienard and .... Farquharson, Captain in Ogilvy's Regiment 1745. [OR3]

SHAW, DUNCAN, son of James Shaw of Crathienard and ... Young, factor to Lord Airlie in Milton of Cortachy, Depute Lord Lieutenant 1745.[LPR234][OR155]

SHAW, JAMES, servant in Dundee, soldier of Ogilvy's Regiment 1745. [OR48]

SHAW, JOHN, son of Duncan Shaw of Crathienard and ... Farquharson, farmer in Ravernie, Lintrathen, Ensign of Ogilvy's Regiment, 1745. [OR7/156]

SHAW, WILLIAM, farmer in Drumfin, Forter, Glen Isla, son of Duncan Shaw of Crathienard and ... Farquharson, Captain of Ogilvy's Regiment 1745, died in Forter 1790. [OR3/157]

SHEPHERD, DAVID, servant in Usan, soldier of Ogilvy's Regiment 1745. [OR49]

SHEPHERD, JOHN, born 1727, inn servant in Ferryden, soldier of Ogilvy's Regiment 1745, a prisoner in Stirling, Leith, Canongate and Carlisle 1746, transported from Liverpool to Virginia on the Gildart 24.2.1747, landed at Port North Potomac, Maryland, 5.8.1747. [OR48][P.3.310][[PRO.T1.328]

SHEPHERD, JOHN, merchant in Brechin, Ensign of Ogilvy's Regiment, 1745. [OR7]

SHEPHERD, WILLIAM, born 1730, sailor on the Samuel and Henry of Dundee 1746, prisoner in Stonehaven, Aberdeen and Canongate 1746. [P3.312]

SHUNGER, JOHN, born 1.6.1725, son of John Shunger in Glamis, ploughman in Glen Ogilvy, soldier of Ogilvy's Regiment 1745, transported 1747.[OR49]

SIMPSON, ANDREW, a sailor in Dundee, drummer of Ogilvy's Regiment 1745, a prisoner in Dundee 1746. [OR8][LPR236]

SIMPSON, DAVID, born 1691, a linen weaver in Auldbar, soldier of Ogilvy's Regiment 1745, prisoner in Dundee, Canongate, and Carlisle, 1746, transported 1747. [P.3.314]

SIMPSON, JAMES, born 1727, shoemaker in Arbroath, soldier of Ogilvy's Regiment 1745, prisoner in Arbraoth, Dundee, Canongate and Carlisle 1746, transported from Liverpool to Virginia on the Johnson 22.4.1747, landed at Port Oxford, Maryland, 5.8.1747. [P.3.314][PRO.T1.328]

SIMPSON, JOHN, servant in Forfar, soldier of Ogilvy's Regiment 1745. [OR49]

SIMPSON, PATRICK, farmer in Mid Dod, Forfar, soldier of Ogilvy's Regiment 1745, prisoner in Montrose 1746. [OR49][P3.314]

SIMPSON, WILLIAM, Episcopal preacher in Dun, deposed 1716. [SRO.CH2.575/1]

SIMPSON, WILLIAM, workman in Forfar, soldier of Ogilvy's Regiment 1745.[OR49]

SINCLAIR, DAVID, prisoner in Perth 1746. [P3.314]

SINCLAIR, JOHN, town piper of Arbroath, piper of Ogilvy's Regiment 1745, prisoner in Arbroath, Stirling and Edinburgh 1746. [P3.316]

SKINNER, JAMES, in Montrose, prisoner in Montrose and Stirling 1746. [P3.318]

SMALL, JOHN, a boy in Dundee, soldier of the Duke of Perth's Regiment 1745, prisoner in Carlisle and Lancaster, transported 1748. [P3.318]

SMART, WALTER, workman in Keithock, Brechin, soldier of Ogilvy's Regiment 1745. [OR49]

SMITH, ALEXANDER, farmer in Boysack Mill, Kinnell, Sergeant of Ogilvy's Regiment 1745, killed. [OR10]

SMITH, ALEXANDER, ploughman in Gilchorn, Inverkeillor, soldier of Ogilvy's Regiment 1745, killed. [OR49]

SMITH, ALEXANDER, born 1720, wigmaker in Montrose, soldier of Ogilvy's Regiment 1745, prisoner at Culloden and Tilbury, discharged. [P3.318]

SMITH, ALEXANDER, barber in Arbroath, soldier of Ogilvy's Regiment 1745, a prisoner at Culloden, possibly transported from Liverpool to Virginia on the Johnson 22.4.1747, landed at Port Oxford, Maryland, 5.8.1747. [OR49][P.3.318][PRO.T1.328]

SMITH, ANDREW, servant in Forfar, soldier of Ogilvy's Regiment 1745. [OR49]

SMITH, DAVID, servant in Forfar, soldier of Ogilvy's Regiment 1745. [OR49]

SMITH, DAVID, sailor in Montrose, soldier of Ogilvy's Regiment 1745, prisoner in Montrose 1746. [OR50][LPR320]

SMITH, GEORGE, wright in Caldhame, Brechin, Lieutenant of Ogilvy's Regiment 1745. [OR5]

SMITH, JAMES, in Panbride, soldier of Ogilvy's Regiment 1745, prisoner in Arbroath 1746. [P3.322]

SMITH, JOHN, blacksmith in Caldhame, Brechin, soldier of Ogilvy's Regiment 1745. [OR50]

SMITH, JOHN, soldier of Ogilvy's Regiment 1745, prisoner at Culloden, died 10.5.1746. [OR50][P3.324]

SMITH, WILLIAM. threadmaker in Arbroath, soldier of Ogilvy's
Regiment 1745, transported from Liverpool to Virginia on the
Gildart 24.2.1747, landed at Port North Potomac, Maryland,
5.8.1747.[PRO.T1.328][OR50]

SOMERVILLE, PETER, born 1732, shoemaker, drummer of Ogilvy's
Regiment 1745, prisoner in Carlisle and Lincoln 1746, transported
from Liverpool to the Leeward Islands on the Veteran 5.5.1747,
liberated and landed on Martinique 6.1747.
[P3.326][PRO.SP36.102]

SOUTAR, JAMES, merchant in Arbroath, prisoner in Arbroath, Dundee
and Canongate 1746. [P3.326]

SOUTAR, WILLIAM, weaver in Dundee, soldier of Ogilvy's Regiment
1745. [OR50]

SOUTH, DAVID, born 1726, soldier of Ogilvy's Regiment 1745, prisoner
in Inverness 1746. [P3.326]

SPALDING, PETER, cordiner in Logie, soldier of Ogilvy's Regiment
1745, prisoner in Carlisle and Chester. [P3.328]

SPARK, JAMES, wright in Montrose, prisoner in Montrose, Stirling and
Edinburgh 1746. [P3.328]

SPEED, GEORGE, servant in Kintrochet, Brechin, soldier of Ogilvy's
Regiment 1745.[OR50]

STARK, ALEXANDER, servant in Forfar, soldier of Ogilvy's Regiment
1745. [OR50]

STARK, THOMAS, born 1729 son of John Stark, soldier of Ogilvy's
Regiment 1745, a prisoner in London. [OR50]

STARK, WILLIAM, weaver in Muir of Meathie, Inverarity, soldier of
Ogilvy's Regiment 1745. [OR50]

STEEL, JAMES, in Arbroath, soldier of Ogilvy's Regiment 1745, prisoner
in Arbroath 1746. [P3.332]

STIVEN, JOHN, workman in Hirdhill, Kirriemuir, soldier of Ogilvy's
Regiment 1745.[OR50]

STIVEN, JOHN, wright in Montrose, sergeant of Ogilvy's regiment 1745,
prisoner in Dundee, Montrose, and Canongate 1746.
[LPR186/320][P3.334]

STIVEN, WILLIAM, born 1731, wine cooper in Dundee, soldier of
Ogilvy's Regiment 1745, prisoner in Carlisle and York 1746,
pardoned when enlisted 1748.   [OR50][P3.332]

STORMONTH, JAMES, of Lednathie, Kirriemuir, Lieutenant of Ogilvy's
Regiment 1745. [OR5/161]

STORMONTH, JAMES, of Kinclune, Pitscandly, the younger, born
2.4.1705 son of Thomas Stormonth and Isobel Hood, Ensign of
Ogilvy's Regiment 1745, transported to the West Indies 1747, died
in St Kitts, cnf. 1761 Edinburgh.
[OR7/163][SRO.CC8.8.118][LPR234]

STORMONT, JAMES, a farmer's son in Glenuig, Kirriemuir, soldier of
Ogilvy's Regiment 1745. [OR50]

STORMONT, JOHN, of Kinwhirie, Kirriemuir, prisoner in Montrose
1746. [LPR236]

STOUTER, JAMES, brewer in Arbroath, soldier of Ogilvy's Regiment
1745. [OR51]

STRACHAN, JOHN, cottar in Cotton of Grange of Kinnell, soldier of
Ogilvy's Regiment, {killed at Culloden?}, prisoner in Dundee 1747.
[OR51][P3.354]

STRACHAN, JOHN, born 1715, butcher in Nether Tenements of
Caldhame, Brechin, prisoner in Montrose, Inverness and Tilbury
1746. [LPR188][P3.354]

STRACHAN, JOHN, servant in Bridgend, Brechin, soldier of Ogilvy's
Regiment 1745.[OR51]

STRACHAN, JOHN, from Brechin, tenant in Kincardine, prisoner in
Aberdeen and Edinburgh 1746. [P3.354]

STRACHAN, ROBERT, merchant in Montrose, prisoner in Montrose and
Stirling 1746. [P3.354]

STRATON, JOHN, Episcopal preacher in Arbirlot 1715. [HHA.170]

STUART, ALEXANDER, gardener in Cookston, Airlie, Sergeant of
Ogilvy's Regiment 1745. [OR10]

STUART, ALEXANDER, merchant in Dundee, 1745, prisoner in Dundee
1746.   [LPR238][OR126][P3.334]

STUART, JAMES, workman in Kingoldrum, soldier of Ogilvy's Regiment
1745. [OR51]

STUART, JAMES, merchant in Montrose, 1745. [LPR186]

STUART, JAMES, porter in Dundee, soldier of Ogilvy's Regiment 1745.
[OR51]

STUART, JOHN, son of James Stuart in Dundee, soldier of Ogilvy's
Regiment 1745.[OR51]

STUBBLE, DAVID, workman in Kettins, soldier of Ogilvy's Regiment
1745. [OR51]

STURROCK, JAMES, farmer in Arbroath, prisoner in Montrose and
Stirling 1746.[P3.356]

SUTHERLAND, ALEXANDER, shoemaker in Montrose, soldier of
Ogilvy's Regiment 1745. [OR51]

TALBOT, JOHN, weaver in Dundee, soldier of Ogilvy's Regiment 1745. [OR51]

TARRAN, JOHN, town officer of Montrose, prisoner in Stirling 1746. [P3.362]

TAYLOR, CHARLES, servant in Glamis, soldier of Ogilvy's Regiment 1745, prisoner in Montrose 1746. [OR51][P3.364]

TAYLOR, ROBERT, in Kirkden, 1715. [HHA170]

TAYLOR, WILLIAM, coachman in Glamis, soldier of Ogilvy's Regiment 1745, prisoner in Montrose 1746. [P3.368] [OR51]

TAYLOR, WILLIAM, brewer in Cotton of Gardyne, Kirkden, soldier of Ogilvy's Regiment 1745, killed at Culloden. [OR52]

THOM, COLIN, born 1703, tailor in Kirriemuir, soldier of Ogilvy's Regiment 1745, prisoner in Montrose, Inverness and Tilbury 1746. [OR52][P3.370]

THOM, GEORGE, workman in Formal, Lintrathen, soldier of Ogilvy's Regiment 1745. [OR52]

THOM, ROBERT, born 1731, labourer in Forfar, soldier of Ogilvy's Regiment 1745, prisoner at Carlisle, York, and Lincoln 1746, transported from Liverpool to the Leeward Islands on the Veteran 5.5.1747 liberated and landed on Martinique 6.1747. [P.3.370][PRO.SP36.102][OR52]

THOMSON, CHARLES, Episcopal preacher in Kinnell 1715. [HHA.170]

THOMSON, JOHN, workman in Wardend, Lintrathen, soldier of Ogilvy's Regiment 1745, escaped from Dundee via Norway to France 1746. [OR52/166]

THOMSON, PATRICK, shoemaker in Dundee, soldier of Ogilvy's Regiment 1745, prisoner in Arbroath, Stirling and Carlisle 1746, transported to Antigua 8.5.1747. [P3.372]

THOMSON, ROBERT, farmer in the Mains of Dun, soldier of Ogilvy's Regiment 1745. [OR52]

THOMSON, WILLIAM, born 1707, workman in Little Kenny, Kingoldrum, soldier of Ogilvy's Regiment 1745, prisoner in Carlisle, York and Lincoln 1746, transported from Liverpool to the Leeward Islands on the Veteran 5.5.1747, liberated and landed on Martinique 6.1747 [OR52][P.3.372][PRO.SP36.102]

TINDAL, COLIN, born 1676, farmer in Nether Pitforthy, Brechin, Sergeant of Ogilvy's Regiment 1745, prisoner in Montrose, Inverness and Tilbury 1746. [OR10][P3.374]

TINDAL, DAVID, tenant farmer in Nether Pitforthy, Brechin, soldier of Ogilvy's Regiment 1745, a prisoner [OR52]

URQUHART, ADAM, Lieutenant of Panmure's Foot, 1715. [SRO.GD45.1.201]

VOLUME, THOMAS, servant in Cossins, Glamis, soldier of Ogilvy's Regiment 1745.[OR52]

WADE, GEORGE, workman in Brechin, soldier of Ogilvy's Regiment 1745. [OR53]

WAGRIE, JOHN, apprentice in Dundee, soldier of Ogilvy's Regiment 1745. [OR53]

WALKER, ROBERT, farmer in Bolshan, Kinnell, Ensign of Ogilvy's Regiment 1745.[OR7]

WALLACE, PATRICK, Provost of Arbroath, 1745. [LPR192]

WALLACE, PATRICK, linen manufacturer and baillie of Arbroath, son of Provost Wallace, merchant in Arbroath, Captain of Ogilvy's Regiment, Governor of Arbroath 1745, a prisoner after Culloden 1746, later in the Tower of London   [OR3/167][P3.388]

WARDEN, JAMES, Town officer of Brechin, Drummer of Ogilvy's Regiment 1745.[OR8]

WATSON, ALEXANDER, of Wallace-Craigie, Depute Governor of Dundee 1745.[LPR238]

WATSON, ALEXANDER, born 1703, soldier of Ogilvy's Regiment 1745, prisoner in   Inverness 1746. [P3.390]

WATSON, DAVID, Episcopal preacher in Fearn, deposed 1716. [SRO.CH2.575/1]

WATSON, JAMES, Episcopal preacher in Kinnell 1715. [HHA170]

WATSON, JAMES, cottar in Highhouse, Craig, soldier of Ogilvy's Regiment 1745.[OR53]

WATSON, JAMES, labourer in Kettins, soldier of Ogilvy's Regiment 1745. [OR53]

WATSON, JOHN, brewer in Arbroath, soldier of Ogilvy's Regiment 1745, a prisoner at Culloden, Stirling, Leith, Carlisle 1746, transported 1747. [OR53][P.3.392]

WATSON, JOHN, in Turin near Forfar, prisoner in Montrose 1746. [P3.392]

WATSON, THOMAS, tobacconist burgess of Arbroath, son of James Watson tenant farmer in the Mains of Auchmithie, Lieutenant of Ogilvy's Regiment 1745, prisoner at Culloden, Montrose, Inverness, London, 1746, transported 1748. [HHA176][OR5/168][P.3.392]

WATSON, THOMAS, merchant in Kirriemuir, soldier of Ogilvy's Regiment 1745.   [OR53]

WATSON, WILLIAM, servant in Glamis, soldier of Ogilvy's Regiment 1745. [OR53]

WATT, WILLIAM, ploughman in Greenlawhill, Barry, soldier of Ogilvy's Regiment 1745. [OR53]

WEBSTER, ANDREW, wright in Arbroath, soldier of Ogilvy's Regiment 1745, prisoner in Edinburgh 1746. [P3.394][OR53]

WEBSTER, CHARLES, born 1728, workman in Pearsie, Kingoldrum, soldier of Ogilvy's Regiment 1745, a prisoner in Montrose and Carlisle. [OR53][P3.395]

WEBSTER, DAVID, born 1727, joiner in Arbroath, soldier of Ogilvy's Regiment 1745, prisoner in Carlisle and York, pardoned on enlistment 1748.[P3.394]

WEBSTER, GEORGE, from Brechin, soldier of Ogilvy's Regiment 1745, soldier of Ogilvy's Regiment 1745, prisoner in Montrose, Dundee and Edinburgh 1746.   [P3.396]

WEBSTER, GEORGE. workman in Kingoldrum, soldier of Ogilvy's Regiment 1745, prisoner at Derby, Carlisle and York, pardoned on enlistment 1748. [OR53][P3.396]

WEBSTER, JOHN, workman in Forfar, soldier of Ogilvy's Regiment 1745, a prisoner.[OR54]

WEBSTER, JOHN, weaver in Forfar, soldier of Ogilvy's Regiment 1745, prisoner in Montrose 1746. [OR54][P3.396]

WEBSTER, JOHN, from St Vigeans, Chelsea Pensioner in Arbroath, Drill Instructor of Ogilvy's Regiment 1745, a prisoner in Arbroath and Montrose 1746. [OR8][P3.396]

WEBSTER, JOHN, sailor in Arbroath, prisoner in Arbroath and Stirling 1746. [P3.396]

WEBSTER, JOHN, mason in Kirriemuir, Sergeant of Ogilvy's Regiment 1745. [OR10]

WEBSTER, WILLIAM, chapman in Brechin, soldier of Ogilvy's Regiment 1745. [OR54]

WEDDERBURN, ALEXANDER, town clerk of Dundee, deprived of his office 1716.[TRA.TC.CC.1/132]

WEDDERBURN, Sir JOHN, the younger, of Blackness, Nevay, Newtyle, Captain of Ogilvy's Regiment 1745, prisoner at Culloden, Inverness and London 1746, executed 28.11.1746. [OR3][LPR238][P3.396]

WEDDERBURN, JOHN, born 21.2.1729, son of Sir John Wedderburn of Blackness and Jean Fullerton, soldier 1745, escaped to America, later a surgeon in Jamaica, died in Scotland 13.6.1803. [LPR238/239][OR179]

WEDDERBURN, ROBERT, of Pearsie, Kingoldrum, Sheriff Clerk of Forfarshire, died 19.2.1786. [OR181]

WEMYSS, JAMES, skipper in Broughty Ferry, prisoner in Dundee and Edinburgh 1746. [P3.398]

WHITE, ALEXANDER, servant in Cleppithill, Mossend, Glamis, soldier of Ogilvy's Regiment 1745. [OR54]

WHITE, JAMES, workman in Wester Lednathie, Kirriemuir, soldier of Ogilvy's Regiment 1745. [OR54]

WHITE, JOHN, workman in Kinclune, Kingoldrum, soldier of Ogilvy's Regiment 1745. [OR54]

WILKIE, DAVID, workman in Coreffie, Lintrathen, soldier of Ogilvy's Regiment 1745, a prisoner in Carlisle and York, pardoned on enlistment 1748. [OR54][P3.402]

WILKIE, GEORGE, farmer's son in Auchlishie, Kirriemuir, soldier of Ogilvy's Regiment 1745. [OR54]

WILKIE, GEORGE, apprentice merchant in Dundee, soldier of Ogilvy's Regiment 1745. [OR54]

WILKIE, JOHN, servant in Forfar, soldier of Ogilvy's Regiment 1745. [OR54]

WILKIE, JOHN, workman in Nether Campsie, Lintrathen, soldier of Ogilvy's Regiment 1745. [OR54]

WILKIE, THOMAS, skipper in Arbroath, prisoner there 1746. [P3.402]

WILLIAMSON, DAVID, merchant in Dundee, prisoner there 1746. [LPR238] [P3.402]

WILLIAMSON, JOHN, cooper in Dundee, soldier of Ogilvy's Regiment 1745, prisoner in Carlisle and Lancaster 1746, transported from Liverpool to the Leeward Islands on the Veteran 8.5.1747, liberated and landed on Martinique 6.1747. [P3.402][PRO.SP36.102] [OR54]

WILLIAMSON, WILLIAM, shoemaker in Montrose, soldier of Ogilvy's Regiment 1745, prisoner there 1746. [OR55][LPR320] [P3.404]

WILLOX, CHARLES, born 1713 son of Walter Willox and Agnes Belly, mason in Upper Tenements of Caldhame, Brechin, soldier of Ogilvy's Regiment 1745, prisoner in Montrose, Inverness and Tilbury 1746. [LPR194][P3.404]

WILSON, DAVID, brewer in Arbroath, soldier of Ogilvy's Regiment 1745.[OR55]

WILSON, DAVID, weaver in Cotton of Lour, soldier of Ogilvy's Regiment 1745.[OR55]

WILSON, JAMES, workman in Inchbraughty, Kirriemuir, soldier of Ogilvy's Regiment 1745. [OR55]

WILSON, JOHN, son of Thomas Wilson in Tarrie, St Vigeans, Hussar 1745. [LPR192]

WILSON, THOMAS, workman in Craigiemaig, Kirriemuir, soldier of Ogilvy's Regiment 1745. [OR55]

WILSON, ..., son of a former officer, near Dundee, soldier of Ogilvy's Regiment 1745. [OR55]

WINTER, ..., in Tannadice, soldier of Ogilvy's Regiment 1745. [OR55]

WINTON, WILLIAM, weaver in Craigton, Monikie, soldier of Ogilvy's Regiment 1745. [OR55]

WISHART, ALEXANDER, in Farnell, soldier of Ogilvy's Regiment 1745, prisoner in Montrose 1746. [P3.400]

WISHART, ALEXANDER, born 29.8.1725 son of John Wishart and Isobel Lawson, a servant in Montrose, transported from London to Jamaica on the St George or the Carteret 19.3.1747, landed in Jamaica 1747. [P.3.400][PRO.CO137.58]

WISHART, JOHN, merchant in Dundee, Lieutenant of Ogilvy's Regiment 1745.[OR5]

WOOD, WILLIAM, mason in Dundee, soldier of Ogilvy's Regiment 1745. [OR55]

WOOD, ..., of Allardie, St Vigeans, soldier of Ogilvy's Regiment 1745. [OR55]

WRIGHT, JOHN, workman in Kingoldrum, soldier of Ogilvy's Regiment 1745. [OR55]

WRIGHT, JOHN, servant in Lindertis, Airlie, soldier of Ogilvy's Regiment 1745.[OR56]

WRIGHT, ROBERT, shoemaker in Montrose, soldier of Ogilvy's Regiment 1745, prisoner there. [LPR192/320] [OR56][P3.410]

WYLLIE, FRANCIS, servant in Powmill, Farnell, soldier of Ogilvy's Regiment 1745. [OR55]

WYLLIE, JAMES, born 1695, soldier of Ogilvy's Regiment 1745, prisoner in Inverness 1746. [P3.412]

YOULLY, DAVID, weaver in Newbigging, Newtyle, soldier of Ogilvy's Regiment 1745. [OR56]

YOUNG, ALEXANDER, workman in Balintore, Lintrathen, soldier of Ogilvy's Regiment 1745. [OR56]

YOUNG, ALEXANDER, sailor in Montrose, soldier of Ogilvy's Regiment 1745, prisoner in Montrose 1746. [LPR320][OR56]

YOUNG, DAVID, weaver in Newbigging, Newtyle, soldier of Ogilvy's Regiment 1745. [OR56]

YOUNG, JAMES, servant in Dundee, soldier of Ogilvy's Regiment 1745. [OR56]

YOUNG, ROBERT, farmer in Leuchland, Brechin, Captain of Ogilvy's Regiment 1745. [OR3/183]

YOUNG, WALTER, born Inverkeillor 1720, sailor in Montrose, Sergeant of Ogilvy's Regiment 1745, a prisoner in Montrose, Inverness and Tilbury 1746. [OR10][P3.414]

YOUNG, WALTER, soldier of Ogilvy's Regiment 1745, a prisoner at Carlisle 1745. [OR56][P3.414]

Lightning Source UK Ltd.
Milton Keynes UK
UKHW01f2152130818
327178UK00010B/466/P